7 STEPS TO GLOBAL ECONOMIC AND SPIRITUAL TRANSFORMATION

"… and Jesus went into the temple … and overthrew the tables of the money changers … And he taught … 'Is it not written that my house shall be called of all nations the house of prayer? But ye have made it a den of thieves.'"
-- Mark 11:15-17

Thou shalt not lend upon interest to thy brother: interest of money, interest of victuals, interest of any thing that is lent upon interest. -- Deuteronomy 23:20-21

If you have money, do not lend it at interest, but give it to one from whom you will not get it back. --The Gospel of Thomas (95). (The Gospel of Thomas (and other texts found at Nag Hammadi [*Gnostic Gospels*] and Qumran [*Dead Sea Scrolls*]) predates the text that were edited and synthesized by Bishop Irenaeus of Lyon (3rd Century CE) and the Council of Nicaea (4th Century CE) to form what is currently used as the Christian *Bible*.)

Those who charge usury are in the same position as those controlled by the devil's influence. This is because they claim that usury is the same as commerce. However, God permits commerce, and prohibits usury. Thus, whoever heeds this commandment from his Lord, and refrains from usury, he may keep his past earnings, and his judgment rests with God. As for those who persist in usury, they incur Hell, wherein they abide forever. --*Qur'an*, Al-Baqarah 2:275

7 STEPS TO GLOBAL ECONOMIC AND SPIRITUAL TRANSFORMATION

BY

ROBERT BOWS

RABBONAI PRESS
Boulder, Colorado

Other books by Robert Bows

Solomon's Proof—A Psycho-Spiritual Journey to World Consciousness, **by Rashan Barcusé (pseudonym)**

N.B.: When using the hyperlinks in the footnotes of this book, be aware that some browsers block progressive websites. We recommend finding a browser that operates independent of corporate censors.

Table of Contents

PREFACE

I don't think there is a great fiction that is not an essential contradiction of the world as it is. … This is the great contribution of the novel to human progress. You know, the Inquisition forbade the novel for 300 years in Latin America. I think they understood very well the seditious consequence that fiction can have on the human psyche. —Mario Vargas Llosa, 2010 Nobel laureate in literature, in an interview in The New York Times, *2002*

The origins of this book

My first book, *Solomon's Proof*,[1] begins with a conversation—between fictionalized versions of the author, who is represented as an accountant and budding playwright, and a friend, a successful writer and editor in New York City—regarding the fine line between fiction and non-fiction, especially when it comes to exploring the interplay of our own psychological and spiritual forces.

This may seem like an arcane point from the past to bring forward in this book about global transformation, but unless we understand such things about ourselves—the workings of our minds below the level of consciousness—then there is little point in trying to distinguish between objectivity and subjectivity, or science and myth, since we would not know when we were fooling ourselves.

Yet science, considered by many to be the ultimate arbiter of logic and perception, now tells us, through the lens of quantum theory, that at the

---

[1] Rashan Barcusé (pseudonym), *Solomon's Proof—A Psycho-Spiritual Journey to World Consciousness*, Rabbonai Press, Boulder, CO, 2008. Available online through Amazon and other vendors.

most basic levels of creation, there is no such thing as certainty. As Heisenberg so ably noted regarding his famous principle, even science must come to grips with uncertainty regarding light (quanta), from which everything in the universe is made. In other words, anomalies are part of the fabric of the universe.

By the end of *Solomon's Proof*, the protagonist, the higher self of the author—a yoga teacher, social theorist, and writer—having reconciled these disparate psychological and spiritual elements within, and having come to grips with his own subjective and objective states, encourages others to undertake a similar journey in the interest of human evolution.

To paraphrase:

> The current dominant paradigm, the route by which instincts and ego rule, in which materialism tyrannizes and greed is celebrated, leads directly to the slavery of the vast majority of humankind, the destruction of our biosphere, and the end of human life on earth.
>
> Altering our destructive course begins within. Individually, we must choose a different path, one uniquely our own. Each of us must discover our gift, develop it, and then join together with others in sharing our gifts. In this way, we shall transform the world.

Nine years after suggesting the aforesaid, I offer this sequel, along the lines of what I asked others to take to heart: discover your gift, develop it, and share it with others. But this iteration of my prescription is, in a literary and literal sense, a horse of different color. The psycho-spiritual integration of the self, from *Solomon's Proof*, has given way to what Buddhists call "right action," which stems from the root truths unveiled during one's personal transformative process, much like a Native American vision quest or a yogic rebirth. As a result—and abandoning the pseudonymous conceit of my first book—my narrative voice and *nom de plume* shift from my lower self to my integrated self and given name, thus inhabiting the transformation that I prescribe.

In this case, a personal transformation means applying the principles of light, as they are delineated in our Quantum-Torus Model at www.solomonsproof.com, to redefine the economic, political, and spiritual framework of the past into a new paradigm, to meet the extraordinary demands at this decisive nexus in human history.

Where the psycho-spiritual memoir of *Solomon's Proof* defines the next step in human evolution in broad terms, we hope that this follow-up volume contributes to the formative details of and blueprint for the monumental shift we must undertake as a species: to thrive in a sustainable, progressive, and spiritual manner on this planet.

To this end, we believe that defining the forces which now suppress human evolution, and clarifying the actions that human beings must self-consciously undertake to bring about personal and collective growth, are the most effective tasks that we can undertake at this time.

It is our hope that what you read here will inspire you to discover your own unique gift, develop it, and share it with others. In this way, we shall transform ourselves and the world.

INTRODUCTION

> *"The citizen who thinks he sees that the commonwealth's political clothes are worn out, and yet holds his peace and does not agitate for a new suit, is disloyal, he is a traitor. That he may be the only one who thinks he sees this decay, does not excuse him: it is his duty to agitate anyway, and it is the duty of others to vote him down if they do not see the matter as he does." —Mark Twain, A Connecticut Yankee in King Arthur's Court, 1889, Ch. 13.*

Economic and spiritual transformation

Humanity is at its crossroads. The evidence is undeniable: human populations, driven by self-subscribed consumption demands, are not only destroying the environment—including air, water, and arable land—but are destroying each other in competition for the natural resources needed to sustain their over-consumption.

Over-consumption is both an economic and spiritual problem: it is economic because it demands that labor and commerce produce and distribute goods and services to satisfy its appetite; it is spiritual because our current level of demand represents instinctive and egoistic impulses untempered by our higher nature and out of synch with Mother Nature's renewable capacities.

There has always been a segment of humankind that questions the existence of our higher nature, leveraging their mechanistic, cause and effect view of phenomena to marginalize any thoughts of the greater good. Until recently it was only possible to counter such pseudo-scientific reasoning with intuitive arguments that fall short of empirical proof; however, such empirical proof is now available, as we see in the framework provided by Solomon's Proof.[2]

Solomon's Proof, based on an interrelated body of scientific theories, data, and observations[3] generated by the unfolding work of contemporary physicists and mathematicians, shows that everything in the universe emanates from the same point of origin and returns back to it: the Singularity, or unified field—an anomalistic state of matter[4] in which the entire universe is undifferentiated; that is, not comprised of similar molecules, atoms, or sub-atomic particles, but consisting of the very same uniform state throughout.[5]

This Singularity is what we intuit as omnipresence, the root of all spiritual and religious experience. It is the unitary 1st dimension in which science and spirituality converge: the supreme state of being, an anomaly from which the infinite potentiality of the universe unfolds— first as duality (wave and particle, light and darkness, etc.),[6] and then

---

[2] Solomon's Proof is posted and updated at http://solomonsproof.com/. The implications of the proof, as the self-described "framework for the final theory," are developed in the novel, *Solomon's Proof*, available online at Amazon, Barnes & Noble, and other sites.

[3] Einstein's Theory of Relativity, Heisenberg's Uncertainty Principle, Gamow's Big Bang Theory, Poincaré's Conjecture, String Theory, action-at-a-distance, etc. Also, consider John Hagelin's comments in the video "It's Time to Wake Up – We Are All One" (http://www.youtube.com/watch?v=pIJHJzDQcRM) at 6:16 and following.

[4] The contrapositive, if you will, of the Bose-Einstein Condensate that exists at or near Absolute Zero, at the other end of the energy excitation scale.

[5] This does not preclude a model of the universe as "continuous creation," that is, one which cycles through Singularity, big bang expansion (white hole) folding back on itself into contraction (via toroidal motion), which leads to a black hole that eventually returns to Singularity, etc., ad infinitum.

[6] That is, the so-called Big Bang theory, which follows the same pattern as Genesis. See Schroeder, Gerald L., *Genesis and the Big Bang: The Discovery Of Harmony Between Modern Science And The Bible*, Bantam, New York, 1991.

in additional dimensions.[7]

Solomon's Proof reveals the intrinsic logic and framework of this sequencing, from the origins of the universe to the next (3rd major) step in human evolution, which is nothing less than light becoming conscious of itself; that is, overcoming the tyranny of the instincts and ego, and unfolding into what the proof terms "conscious spiritual evolution"—a logical progression from the two preceding key steps in human development: (1) standing erect, i.e., "unconscious physical evolution," and (2) mastering symbolic forms (language, music, mathematics, etc.), i.e., "subconscious mental evolution."

To create an economically sustainable and spiritually evolved society—which reflects this progression of universal forces[8]—requires a self-consciousness act on the part of each individual; in other words, each of us adopting a spiritual practice that empowers our higher nature. Such a practice may consist of anything on the scale from learning to take a deep breath and counting to ten, whenever circumstances require, to undertaking a full-fledged yoga practice that encompasses each of the traditional eight steps; or, alternatively, taking up some in-between practice, any of a host of proven techniques designed to overcome the tyranny of the instincts and the ego.

In any case, the self-conscious global transformation that we seek is both economic and spiritual.

The development and objective of this thesis

As Solomon's Proof shows, human beings are a refined evolutionary development of light—light conscious of itself—and, as such, have a great deal more power than they are aware. Every one of us is an

---

[7] Each dimension—1-D (Singularity), 2-D, 3-D, 4-D, and beyond—is subject to its own rules. For example: 2-D is governed by the rules of plane geometry; 3-D is governed by solid geometry; 4-D by topology: etc.

[8] All matter being derived from light (quanta).

emanation of the indefinable force that animates creation; yet, the illusion of our separateness, fostered by the instincts and ego and their hormonal components,[9] has dominated humankind's behavior for much of its history, despite our nurturing and contemplative capacities.

One of the key ways in which this illusion of separateness propagates itself, like *The Matrix* in the film of the same name, is by valuing human activity and culture in terms of money-as-a-commodity—such as capital, gold and silver, or oil—instead of valuing human activity and culture for their own sake, first and foremost, and by making these activities the true measure of value.

When we value money over people, we enable an abstraction to rule over us and suppress our nature, rather than self-directing the value that we create, by our labor,[10] to further our own development.

In this way, money, in its commodified form as capital—and the psychological and emotional imperatives that are presently bound to it—has become the principle obstacle to economic and spiritual transformation. Despite its ubiquity, money remains one of the least understood forces in our world; yet, the proper use of money being inextricably bound to our spiritual transformation makes our understanding of it doubly important.

Thus, *Step 1—Exposing the story of money and usury* explores how money is transformed from the value created by labor into a commodity (capital), whenever money creation is privately controlled. In this way, labor becomes a commodity via interest, which usurps the fruits of labor. This is why Judaism, Christianity, and Islam all oppose usury.

In *Step 2—Rejecting the false divisions of ethnicities, religions, political parties, and nationalities*, we dissect some of the most

---

[9] The fight or flight syndrome defined by aggression and fear.

[10] In addition to work, labor includes the creation and use of manual tools, machines, computers, and robots that produce goods and services.

insidious disinformation generated around these topics, beginning with the way in which religion has perverted spiritual teachings to justify the primacy of private wealth over the commonwealth.

A key factor in our ability to discredit and defuse such propaganda is to raise awareness of the nature of the powers-that-be and their objectives. In *Step 3—Transposing the money cartel's point-of-view*, we piece together the *modus operandi* of those who control the corporate banking pyramid scheme. Understanding the world from this vantage point allows us to see how issues have been manufactured to divide us and distract us from the root cause of global dysfunction— private control over money creation—and how this has enabled control over the planet by a handful of families.

When we are no longer divided by illusory differences, we are free to reorganize our resources into relationships that serve the commonwealth. *Step 4 —Making money a public utility through sustainable economics*, explains the principles by which publicly owned banks have thrived through the centuries in places as diverse as Australia, Venice, Guernsey, Libya, Germany, Switzerland, and North Dakota. The secret to this success is simple: the profits of the bank are returned to the general fund of the public body (nation, state, county, and/or city), to be spent into the economy, or used to increase credit on "Main Street," rather than having it siphoned off by "Wall Street," which serves over-consumption and the lust of power for a handful of persons. In delineating the differences between the system of privately controlled banks, currency, and credit versus a publicly owned monetary system, we prove that the only truly sustainable model is money as a public utility, just as Aristotle noted, where interest and private banks are permanently retired, enabling stable currency value and commodity prices, as well as sustainable economies, as the rule.

However, publicly owned banks, in and of themselves, are not sufficient to bring about the great economic and spiritual transformation that is our evolutionary birthright. Democratic societies cannot exist without a free, decentralized press and verifiable elections. The requirements for these functions are detailed in *Step 5 —Restoring democracy.*

Before we conclude by exploring our personal options, we must pause and take notice of the ravages that surround us. In *Step 6 —Restoring Law, Science, and Logic*, we consider how the banking cartel came to control the legal system, empirical endeavors, and thought itself. Understanding this, we then offer a strategy for the re-establishment of law and scientific method governed by the power of reasoning, rather than the exigencies of capital.

This leads us to our conclusion, *Step 7—Taking humanity's next step*, a discussion of the intrinsic economic and spiritual implications of light as it progresses from the origins of the universe to universal consciousness. Finally, in the last section of this concluding chapter, we look at how each of us, singularly and collectively, can contribute to this evolutionary economic and spiritual transformation.

Humanity at its crossroads: Your role

Above and beyond the key societal dynamics of economics and spirituality explicated in this book, there are a variety of other critical functions, such as education, agriculture, transportation, etc., that must be transformed as well. For the outcome of our current crisis be positive, it will take self-conscious acts on the part of many people— each discovering, developing, and sharing their unique gifts. Despite the emotional, mental, and spiritual artifacts that hold back portions of humanity in previous evolutionary stages, as an ever-greater portion of humanity frees itself from its self-imposed limitations, we shall consequently create the conditions that accelerate this transformation.

Prepare to change yourself and join with others to make this global evolution happen.

PROLOGUE

"Of course we will have fascism in America, but we will call it democracy!" —Huey Long

The author's credentials

As the U.S. moved past the charade of the 2016 U.S. Presidential nomination and election process—and as we waded through the near endless promulgation of fake news,[11] propaganda, and pedestrian analysis, as well as a tsunami of ignorance, misdirection, logical fallacies, and "limited hangout"[12] in the mass and social media—we are compelled to provide advice, distilled from nearly a half-century of applying the lessons of political science and economics that we first learned at Stanford University, in the classroom and in the streets, during those tumultuous times of the late '60's, protesting the war in Vietnam and U.S. imperialism, all of which carried us forward—through decades of political activism, research, and public debate—to the present.

---

[11] By this, we mean principally the agit-prop released by the CIA, FBI, and other intelligence agencies, as well as the corporate-controlled mass and social media, and their click-bait sites.

[12] "Limited hangout" is a term used by intelligence agencies to describe a particular type of propaganda that they generate to mislead target populations by mixing disparate facts (which have already been compromised) with lies, to direct the focus away from the actual facts and perpetrators. It is only one of various PSYOPS techniques used to control populations.
https://info.publicintelligence.net/USArmy-PsyOpsTactics.pdf. The U.S., as proxy for the Anglo-Euro-American banking cartel, has a specific strategy regarding the use of PSYOPS to achieve the objectives of the .000001%:
https://www.thelastamericanvagabond.com/top-news/journalist-eva-bartlett-travels-north-korea-brings-back-photos-different-msm/. Within this environment of deliberate lies, the media is a lethal weapon used to enslave target populations.

This body of work includes a home rule charter and various public laws for the smallest independent municipality in Colorado. Among these legal templates are prescriptions for governing the use of water, as well as elections, aspects of which were adopted by Boulder County, which in turn greatly influenced the vote-by-mail movement in the U.S., before the system was subsequently and thoroughly hijacked via electronic voting and counting systems.[13]

In addition to these examples of political and economic frameworks for municipalities and counties, we helped found Colorado Public Television, and worked as the station manager there, as well as a producer, writer, and director—production roles which we later reprised at Rocky Mountain PBS. Our career as a journalist also includes broadcast radio, cable TV, newspapers, magazines, and web-based content and multimedia.

This was followed in 2010 by serving as one of five founders of the Public Banking Institute, which successfully initiated a movement that, in a few short years, generated legislation for publicly owned banks being introduced in over 20 states and many municipalities. Closer to home, this led to our founding Colorado Public Banking, which, four times, brought the question of a state-owned bank through the initiative process, to be denied each time by the executive, legislative, and judicial branches of the Colorado state government, as detailed in our blog.[14]

Whether or not such cumulative expertise is valued by average laypersons any more than the opinions that they hold—based on their beliefs that the narratives, political preferences, and litanies with which they have been inculcated since birth—remains to be seen; but, at a minimum, we publish this for those responsible for the more than

---

[13] The refusal of various states and the federal judiciary to carry out credible recounts requested by the Stein campaign in 2016 speak volumes about the corruption of our electoral system and judiciary.

[14] http://coloradopublicbanking.blogspot.com/

150,000 page views, over the past few years,[15] of our blog, where many of the ideas presented in this book were first published.

A note on modeling, empirical reasoning, and open minds

As a founder of two public banking organizations, as an activist in monetary reform, and as a reasonably successful blogger, I am often asked to give presentations. These usually begin with a slide that shows two models of our solar system, one created by Tycho Brahe and one created by Nicolaus Copernicus.

Solar System

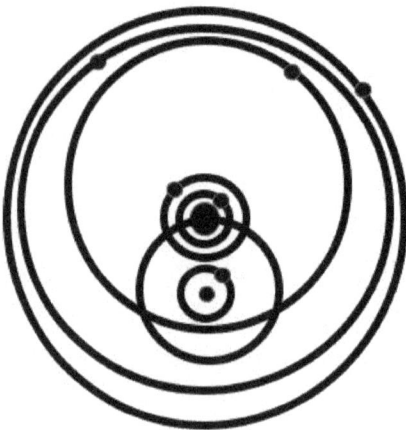

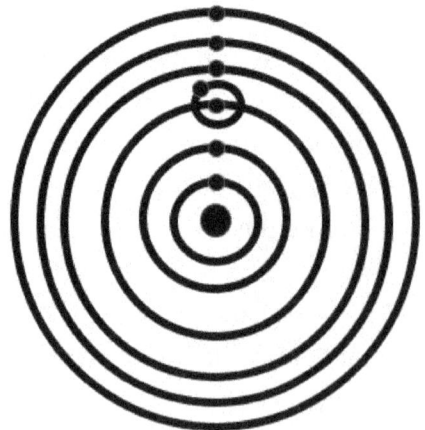

Tychovian   Copernican

Both the Tychovian geocentric system (in which the Sun and the planets rotate around Earth, and which requires the Sun, Mercury, and

---

[15] January 2013 through 2017, despite the drastic suppression of progressive websites, beginning in April 2017. https://popularresistance.org/newsletter-dissent-under-attack-by-government-corporations/

Venus to occasionally wander outside the orbit of Mars) and the Copernican heliocentric system are accurately predictive; which obviously proves that just because a model is accurately predictive does not mean that it accurately represents nature, or that it is the most efficient means for solving a problem. The larger point here is one of the cornerstones of empirical reasoning: All relevant data must be considered; otherwise, the analysis is unscientific and illogical.

For example, while Brahe's model was able to foretell, at any given time, the position of the Sun and the planets, it's flaws became apparent as further mathematical and astronomical evidence appeared.

Interestingly, in *Step 4* of this book, I use a series of graphs based on concentric circles (similar to the Copernican model) to prove this point: that a privately owned banking system, based on profiting from the manipulation of the money supply, is inherently inflationary and unstable, and that a publicly owned banking system, in which usury is prohibited, can easily create a sustainable economy and stable currency value.

While I understand that anyone, whose orientation is inside of the capitalist silo, may have a difficult time accepting the simplicity of what I'm presenting, that is the point of the quote at the top of *Step 1*, which follows this Prologue. So, if you, the reader, are truly interested in alternatives to the present system, you must step outside of your comfortable and seemingly sensible predictive box, and attempt to understand where different, more comprehensive premises may take you.

The 2016 U.S. election as an indicator of global distress

Before we begin our detailed account of the seven learning objectives that humanity must achieve to evolve in a progressive and sustainable manner, it's worth noting some of the key lessons that emerged from the 2016 election season, as these events serve as telling examples of how the system operates and how, given the many levers of control, the powers-that-be are able to fluidly adapt and alter their strategy in response to changes on the ground.

Once the analyses of the independent[16] exit polls versus the reported vote arrived, we were able to see that the results of the blue primary were rigged for Clinton, in at least 12 states,[17] with the red party presidential primary relatively untainted, other than the corporate-controlled media extolling Trump's candidacy at that time, literally foisting him upon red voters, while the corporate-controlled polls cooked the numbers to generate momentum.

As the WikiLeaks DNC emails show, the blue party plan from the beginning was to support, as first choice, a Trump bid, to make Clinton look like the lesser of two evils,[18] and sure enough, when it came to the actual campaign, the Anglo-Euro-American banking cartel—which controls the media, polls, and electronic voting machines—had Trump playing the part of an ignorant buffoon, dutifully sticking his foot in his mouth multiple times each day, in synch with the "news" cycle.

But the release by WikiLeaks of those *leaked* emails, provided by insiders at the DNC and Department of State,[19] made Clinton's

---

[16] The cartel's mass media election analysis includes "normalizing" exit polls; i.e., adjusting them to match the reported vote. Thus, their claim that the exit polls do not show red flags (greater than 2% deviation from the vote) is a tautology (defining their argument to be true).

[17] http://trustvote.org/latest-updates/vote-fractionalizing-and-election-theft/ and http://www.opednews.com/articles/CA-Exit-Polls-reveal-23-D-by-Stephen-Fox-21st-Century-Tammany-Hall-New-York_Andrew-Jackson_Bernie-Sanders-2016-Presidential-Candidate_Brooklyn-And-Bronx-Disenfranchisement-160615-269.html

[18] http://coloradopublicbanking.blogspot.com/2016/06/the-plan-from-beginning-was-lesser-of.html

[19] We reject claims by the CIA that Russia played any role in this, since they have presented no evidence and have a long history, as well as an organizational directive, to create misdirection via propaganda; while, the two men most familiar

appointment untenable, given the criminal evidence that the emails contain (even if she is never indicted, as is always the case with top-level operatives in any system run by private bank holding companies and their corporations,[20] unless these operatives cross their puppet masters).

Regardless, whether Clinton was the cartel's choice from the beginning, or whether Trump was their hidden pick (in the general election, all five swing states were hacked in his favor), makes little difference, given the long-standing control over the executive branch cabinet (be it during Bush, Obama, Trump, or many of their predecessors) by representatives of the "too big to fail" (TBTF) banks that own the Federal Reserve System.

Yet, despite all this, during the worst political season on record, in terms of the obvious degradation of the façade of a presumably democratic republic, the transparency of criminal actions by the red and blue parties and their candidates has served to educate millions of people as to the nature of the planetary power structure. Our hope is that this will feed a politically independent movement capable of overcoming the forces of devolution, and to bring about the necessary steps for human progress.

To this effort, we dedicate this book.

---

with the delivery of the Democratic National Committee (DNC) emails, Julian Assange of WikiLeaks and Craig Murray, the former UK ambassador to Uzbekistan, say that they know the individual who passed along the emails and that he has no connection to Russia. We dissect the "report" of the then National Director of Intelligence, James Clapper at:
http://coloradopublicbanking.blogspot.com/2017/01/us-intelligence-reports-fail.html
[20] http://coloradopublicbanking.blogspot.com/2015/02/the-running-tab-on-bank-fraud.html

Step 1—Exposing the Story of Money and Usury

"If economists can't say what they mean in simple, clear terms, then either there is something to be gained from mystifying what they are doing, or they themselves do not really understand what they claim to understand."
—*Rosa Luxemburg*

"If all economists were laid end to end, they would not reach a conclusion." —George Bernard Shaw[21]

Why start with money?

There is a reason that economics is shrouded in mystery, wrapped in complex terminology, and made to feel outside of our reach; for, to paraphrase Henry Ford,[22] if it were generally known how money works and how control over its creation has led directly to our present global crisis, there would a revolution tomorrow.

Why? Because, once the cloak of disinformation regarding the prevailing economic system is lifted, we find that much of the world's troubles—scarcity, ignorance, disease, and war—are all manufactured to enrich a handful of people.

---

[21] In addition to being a Nobel Laureate in literature, for his playwriting, Shaw was one of the founders of the London School of Economics.

[22] Ford himself was paraphrased in the article "In the Mercury's Opinion: How Internationalists Gain Power," by Russell Maguire in *American Mercury*, (October 1957), p. 79, as: "It is well enough that the people of the nation do not understand our banking and monetary system for, if they did, I believe there would be a revolution before tomorrow morning."

So pervasive is our ignorance of money that we must address its creation before we can address the full scope of the harm that it does to us when it is owned by private interests, as it is now.

Where did money come from?

As David Graeber points out in *Debt: The First 5,000 Years*,[23] anthropologists have challenged the concept promoted by economists that barter was a standard means of exchange before there was money. And while one could argue that anthropological evidence has its own self-imposed prejudices—including the concept that the development of human societies is accurately reflected in the scant evidence that has been collected, particularly concerning Paleolithic groups—for our purposes it makes little difference whether barter did or did not act as a steppingstone toward the creation of money.

The important point is that when money became widespread, it took on a life of its own, affecting us in ways we did not understand and playing a large role in changing human consciousness, culture, and organization, for better and for worse.

This brings us to our present situation, a crossroads similar to when we invented money. It is a time filled with uncertainty and all sorts of problems that need fixing.

While the past has provided us with many valuable lessons, we caution those who would point to prior theories and customs as a means to meet our challenges, which require evolutionary solutions.

> "We shall require a substantially new manner of thinking if mankind is to survive."—Albert Einstein

---

[23] David Graeber, *Debt: The First 5,000 Years*, Melville House Publishing, Brooklyn, NY, 2011.

Is there a better way to use money?

Let's take a closer look at how we got here and see if—by understanding what money is—we can figure out a better way to make money work for us.

What does money stand for?

Generally speaking, money stands for value, either positive or negative: your overall monetary value (net worth) is positive when the money and assets you own, plus the money and assets owed to you by persons or corporations, is greater than what you owe; and, your overall monetary value is negative when the money you owe to persons or corporations is greater than the money and assets you own plus what you are owed. If you are owed no money and you owe no money, then whatever money and assets you have on hand represent an overall positive monetary value.

Where does value come from?

The value that we assign to money is created from labor, or work, including the extraction of natural resources and use of automated production based upon technology (e.g., machines, computers, robots, and artificial intelligence) invented through labor. Without human labor, there is no value. This is generally referred to as the labor theory of value. As we shall show, there is no theory involved; rather, it is a self-conscious choice to put human beings (labor and society), rather than money (capital and cartels), at the center of our economic and spiritual organization. Our choices create the society in which we live.

President Abraham Lincoln put it this way:

> "Labor is prior to, and independent of, capital. Capital is only the fruit of labor, and could never have existed if labor had not first existed. Labor is the superior of capital, and deserves much

3

the higher consideration."[24]

Benjamin Franklin, arguably the greatest promoter for the issuance of sovereign paper currency in the original 13 colonies, thought along similar lines:

> "The riches of a country are to be valued by the quantity of labor its inhabitants are able to purchase and not by the quantity of gold and silver they possess. ... Trade in general being nothing else but the exchange of labor for labor, the value of all things is, as I have said before, most justly measured by labor."[25]

Aristotle posited similar ideas, regarding our choice in defining money, 2000 years earlier:

> "There should be a unity as measure that connects everything and this unity is the basic need. By agreement money represents the need and has its value not by nature, but by law. We can create it, change it, and put it out of circulation. Using money should work according to proportionality—this way all will receive what they need. Need connects people and organizes exchange of work and goods." —Aristotle, *Nicomachean Ethics*

Essentially, credit is nothing more than the promise of future labor, while debits represent labor that has been performed, and interest is labor appropriated and devalued.

Labor is devalued through interest

---

[24] Annual Address to Congress, Dec. 3, 1861. (*Selections from the Letters, Speeches, and State Papers of Abraham Lincoln, by Abraham Lincoln,* edited by Ida Minerva Tarbell, Ginn & Company, 1911, p. 77.)

[25] Benjamin Franklin, *A Modest Enquiry into the Nature and Necessity of a Paper-Currency,* 1729.

Lincoln and Franklin are pointing to the same truth, something also recognized by other notable economists, including Marx, whose assiduous research on the economic activity of the British Empire detailed in his three-volume case study, *Das Kapital*, shows how a system centered on capital must continually expand to survive.

Although profit is an important factor in capitalism, the central dynamic is interest, which instantly turns money (the value created by labor) into a commodity (capital), which in turn is inflated at a compounded rate, devaluing labor proportionally. In other words, at the very moment that interest is charged, things (commodities, including money-as-capital) become valued above people, leading to a variety of aberrations and inverted beliefs and behaviors, such as corporations becoming persons,[26] persons becoming commodities, and money becoming speech.[27]

> "Capitalism reduces labor to a commercial commodity to be traded on the market, rather than a social relationship between people involved in a common effort for survival or betterment."

[26] "Four Corporate Power-Grabs That Got the Thumbs Up from Federal Courts": http://www.alternet.org/corporate-accountability-and-workplace/four-corporate-power-grabs-got-thumbs-federal-courts. Power grab #1; "Corporate Religious Freedom! This notion was recently challenged by a Pennsylvania judge ("Pennsylvania Court Deals Blow to Secrecy-Obsessed Fracking Industry"): http://truth-out.org/news/item/15721-pennsylvania-court-deals-blow-to-secrecy-o); and In PA, the "Corporation Does Not have Natural Personhood": http://portside.org/2013-04-17/pa-corporation-does-not-have-natural-personhood-democracy-coming-usa.

[27] "*Buckley v. Valeo*, 424 US 1 (1976) is US constitutional law case of the US Supreme Court on campaign finance. A majority of judges held limits on election spending in the Federal Election Campaign Act of 1971 §608 were unconstitutional. The majority, in a *per curiam* opinion, contended that expenditure limits contravened the First Amendment provision on freedom of speech because spending money, in its view, was the same as written or verbal expression." (https://en.wikipedia.org/wiki/Buckley_v._Valeo)

–Karl Marx, *Economic and Philosophical Manuscripts of 1844*

Why does value start with human activity?

We attribute value to human activity because, after all, we are the only species that classifies and keeps track of our behavior in this manner— that is, value is a byproduct of our consciousness interacting with our environment. To paraphrase from the famous Confucian tract, the *I Ching*, "the superior person discriminates between high and low." We create and then reflect upon our creation. Value is the importance we place upon that which we have created.

Money, too, is something that we created with our labor. And it is an abstraction that has come to rule us, as we shall see.

How do we trade what we have created?

As our trading of "labor for labor" (to borrow Franklin's phrase) grew, involving greater varieties and numbers of goods and services, so did the use of money. Essentially, money is the lowest common denominator for items with varying values. Depending upon the society, value can be assigned to anything, including people, thereby defining different forms of slavery, including slaves as property and slaves as debtors.

For example, the federal government runs a deficit. This is to be expected, since its operations have been captured by international banking interests, which charge the federal government principal plus interest to use their green pieces of paper (Federal Reserve Notes) to pay its debts. The Anglo-Euro-American banking cartel increases this debt by various means, including wars, "natural" disasters, and economic "collapses," and then collects the interest on the principal via federal income taxes, a mechanism that was created immediately following the passage of the Federal Reserve Act in 1913, for the purpose of paying the interest on the growing debt-to-be, which is

6

bound to increase geometrically via compound interest.[28] No wonder "bankers' hours" are so short, since time is doing most of their "work."

How are money and value related to credit and debt?

Credit is generated by owning, or being owed, things of value; this is the plus side of money, which we sometimes describe as "in the black." Debt is generated by owing things of value, including money; this is the minus side of money, which we sometimes describe as "in the red."

How has the idea of money changed?

In recorded history, we find that money is seen generally in two different ways:

One way of seeing money is as a unit which accounts for value, or as a tally of value; that is, a means of keeping track of credits and debts; for example, a positive bank balance (indicated by a plus sign or black numbers), or a loan statement (indicated by a minus sign or red numbers). In pre-industrial England, matching tally sticks, (split from the same branch) were used for keeping track of credits and debts.

Another way of seeing money is as a store of value; that is, having intrinsic value (as if such a thing were possible outside the sphere of human activity), such as coins made of gold or silver, or when currency is backed by gold and silver bullion, oil, or even a standardized basket of goods. Ultimately, though, the value of these commodities is something that was originally derived from labor. In and of themselves, these commodities have no value except in the context of labor; that is,

---

[28] For example, on a $1000 loan at 10% over 20 years, money lenders receive a 700% ($7000) return. Where does the money come from to pay for the false value ($6,000 in interest) created out of thin air (i.e., not from labor)? It comes out of the existent money supply. Thus, at each succeeding interval in the interest cycle, the banks control an ever-larger percentage of the money supply. More details on this in *Step 4*.

as a result of people working, extracting, employing, and/or purchasing these commodities.[29] As Lincoln and Franklin noted, if people were not present, money (and capital) would not exist, and these various commodities would have no inherent value.

> "For many Ages, those Parts of the World which are engaged in Commerce, have fixed upon Gold and Silver as the chief and most proper Materials for this Medium; they being in themselves valuable Metals for their Fineness, Beauty, and Scarcity. By these, particularly by Silver, it has been usual to value all Things else: But as Silver itself is no certain permanent Value, being worth more or less according to its Scarcity or Plenty, therefore it seems requisite to fix upon Something else, more proper to be made a Measure of Values, and this I take to be Labor." —Benjamin Franklin, *A Modest Enquiry into the Nature and Necessity of a Paper-Currency*, 1729

Money as a unit of accounting for value (a tally of sums earned and owed) predates money as a store of value (a precious metal or commodity) by at least two millennia, and the Sumerian and Egyptian civilizations employing these accounting-entry payment systems lasted thousands of years. This longevity was due, in no small part, to the stability of a system in which the governmental authority creates money, as is needed, to balance and stay proportionate with the value being created by labor (the goods and services in circulation), and is not charged (i.e., it does not charge itself) for its creation or regulation of money. In other words, as a unit of account, money is not treated as a commodity, but rather as value created by labor and managed as a public utility in the public interest. This is the most basic definition of

---

[29] "... Gold and silver are in reality commodities. They are commodities for the attaining of which labor and capital must be employed. It is cost of production, therefore, which determines the value of these, as of other ordinary productions." —*Comments on James Mill's Éléments D'économie Politique*, Karl Marx, 1844, p. 101.

sovereignty: the government, by law, is the only creator of money (legal tender); i.e., a sovereign monetary system exactly as Aristotle prescribed. This is why, during the Middle Ages and Renaissance, the coin of the realm was often called sovereigns, because it was issued by the sovereign entity.

In today's world, money is most often represented as a series of numbers on a privately owned bank's hard drive; yet, despite money's subjective nature, many economists argue that it should be pegged to a single commodity or multiple commodities. But whenever a formal connection between money and commodities is created, it is chiefly for the benefit of speculators and financiers, because the supply of precious metals, minerals, or other valuable commodities cannot expand to match the value of the goods and services that are constantly being created by labor; even worse, the sources of and markets for these precious metals and minerals are monopolized and manipulated by the same folks who control the paper currencies; and worse yet, the brutal conditions under which these commodities are commonly acquired and extracted clearly indicate, once again, that capital is dependent upon human subjugation.

What happens when money as a means of accounting for labor gets confused with money as a commodity?

In medieval Europe, goldsmiths developed a generally secure way of acting as a depository for their customers' gold and other valuables. As a result, they discovered that, at any one time, their customers usually never demanded more than 10% of the total amount of gold and other reserves that were in their vaults.

Observing this pattern enabled the goldsmiths to issue multiple times the amount of loans that they had in gold reserves, enabling their clients to go into debt to them. At this stage, what the goldsmiths were doing was nothing other than counterfeiting; that is, loaning against what they did not own or, in many cases, even have in their possession. Once the goldsmiths amassed enough capital and armed forces financed by their creation of capital, they began to obtain banking franchises from various rulers, which essentially legalized their counterfeiting scam.

At that point, this system of creating money from reserves which do not exist (or exist only in part) became known as "fractional reserve lending." The merchant-customers of the goldsmiths-turned-bankers would set sail with wares purchased with this credit and return with silver or gold, paying off the loans, with a profit for the usurers derived from the interest on the principle of the loan.

Despite the flaws in this system—that the banks were loaning what they didn't have, which often led to economic chaos following runs on the banks (with assets returned for only pennies on the dollar and the perpetrators sometimes hanged or beheaded for abridging the public trust and for the theft of the value created by their labor)—fractional reserve lending allowed European countries to do things that previously were only a wish, such as rapidly expanding their economies and, most notably, helping them come to the understanding that money need not be dependent on or indexed to commodities in order to account for the creation of value by labor, or to steal the value created by labor, as the case may be.

The problem with gold

But in addition to the fallacious notion that currency must be backed by precious metals because such commodities have intrinsic value, the instability and outright criminal operations of privately owned and regulated monetary systems provides another compelling reason for those who reject what the bankers try to pass off as "sound money"; that is, privately owned paper money supposedly backed 100% by gold.

In addition to the spiritual problem of valuing material objects above people, this obsession with precious commodities reveals a lack of understanding regarding the fundamental problems with money as a store of value. Arguments for currencies backed by precious metals generally include the talking point that "the full faith and credit" of a people or nation is an inadequate basis for a currency, failing to mention that an expensive commodity (such as gold), can only be purchased—and thus manipulated—by those who have lots of money or credit, the very people who already own and issue most of the world's currency.

But what is a sovereign currency if not the people, their labor, and the value, or promise of value, they create?

> "Is a Bond or Bill-of-Exchange for £1000, other than paper? And yet is it not as valuable as so much Silver or Gold, supposing the security of Payment is sufficient? Now what is the security of your Paper-money less than the Credit of the whole Country?" —Cotton Mather, *Some Considerations on Bills of Credit*, 1691

We return to our prior quote from Franklin:

> "But as Silver itself is no certain permanent Value, being worth more or less according to its Scarcity or Plenty, therefore it seems requisite to fix upon Something else, more proper to be made a Measure of Values, and this I take to be Labor."— Benjamin Franklin, *A Modest Enquiry into the Nature and Necessity of a Paper-Currency*, 1729

We concur: Labor creates value and the sum total of value is produced by the people, whose labor guarantees it. So, ultimately, the value of labor is represented by currency, which is guaranteed "by the full faith and credit of the people." If there were no people around to back up a currency, then the currency would have neither value nor meaning.

Argentina, during the period from 2001 to 2005,[30] serves as a perfect

---

[30] http://www.voltairenet.org/article167517.html

example of how "the full faith and credit of the people" is the actual value, or promise of value, that backs a currency, and not "fractional reserves" nor vast gold holdings belonging to a small group of persons,[31] who use the illusion of "sound money" to manipulate the system for their advantage.

This demarcation between "the full faith and credit of the people" and the false idols of gold and other material objects appears in almost all spiritual teachings, but it is perhaps best illustrated by the sequence from Exodus in the Torah (what Christianity calls the Old Testament), where Moses returns with the tablets from Mount Sinai and pits faith against the golden calf.

> "They have been quick to turn aside from the way that I commanded them, and have made themselves an idol cast in the shape of a calf. They have bowed down to it and sacrificed to it ..." —*Exodus*, 32:8

Jesus, too, drew the same line in the sand when he said:

> "No man can serve two masters: for either he will hate the one, and love the other; or else he will hold to the one, and despise the other. Ye cannot serve God and mammon." —*Matthew* 6:24

In addition to the spiritual transgression of placing "the value of gold" above that of "faith in people to fulfill their obligations," there are a number of technical factors that undermine the precious metals argument.

As Ellen Brown noted in an interview with the Daily Bell,[32] there are three ways that gold can be integrated into our monetary system:

---

[31] http://www.opednews.com/articles/The-Global-1--Exposing-th-by-Peter-Phillips-120819-734.html and
http://land.netonecom.net/tlp/ref/federal_reserve.shtml
[32] August 23, 2009: http://thedailybell.com/496/Ellen-Brown-Web-of-Debt.html

1. As a "gold-backed" private fiat currency, of the sort we had from 1913 until 1933 domestically, and until 1971 internationally;
2. 100% gold coins; or
3. Gold, silver, and anything else that is traded freely with dollars.

As Brown points out, "the first alternative failed historically and doesn't work mathematically," the second alternative ignores the fact that the amount of gold required is not acquirable, and the third alternative wouldn't change the relative and often volatile exchange of value between paper currency and precious metals, and would be difficult to implement effectively.

For example, consider how quickly the financiers shut down competing private money creation processes (private mints converting gold and silver into coins) during the 19th century mining booms in the American West. After eliminating competing private mints, silver-backed currency was nixed completely (demonetized) a few decades after this, since it is a more difficult market for the banking cartel to monopolize.

In summary, the problem with gold is that, in addition to the spiritual issues (leading to the valuation of a material objects above that of the human community and the biosphere itself), it is a scarce commodity the market for which is cornered[33] by the same small group of financiers (through subjugation, extraction, usury, and central banking) that currently control the money creation process. Whatever gold remains freely circulating at this time is not enough to prevent manipulation of the market by these financiers. In fact, the market is so well-cornered that only the trading is manipulated, not the actual movement of reserves.[34]

---

[33] http://www.zerohedge.com/article/did-gordon-brown-sell-uks-gold-keep-aig-and-rothschild-solvent-more-disclosures-how-ny-fed-m

[34] http://www.telegraph.co.uk/finance/markets/2883029/Rothschild-to-pull-out-

The financiers keep gold in play (through the manipulation of information and markets) to hedge their bets. For example, before they destroy a currency, they take their holdings in that currency and transfer them into precious metals, and then wait until the currency has bottomed out (through their speculation and/or counterfeiting), before converting gold back to the local currency at a geometrically increased share of the money supply, thus enabling their usurpation of local resources.

So, again, we see that the debate on currency boils down to whether our system is going to be based on people or things. Hopefully, it will become obvious to enough people that, when a system is based on gold or on money-as-a-commodity (that is, a store of value, such as capital), the commodities which define value are manipulated for the sake of profiteering,[35] with the rights of people fully abridged and replaced by the rights of corporations. On the other hand, when money is an accounting of the value created by labor, it is sustainable and serves human beings and the biosphere,[36] as we show in *Step 4*.

The problem with interest

While confusing money with commodities is a widespread misconception and practice, the biggest flaw, in the current privately owned banking and monetary system, generally goes unrecognized and is purposefully obfuscated: the interest charged for the use of the financiers' banknotes.

---

of-gold-market-after-200-years.html. The biggest movements of gold reserves since 9-11, have been the thefts of national gold reserves by the cartel via war, following the invasion of Libya and the coup d'état in Ukraine.

[35] As noted by Carl Richards, "It (gold) has no value except the one assigned by a herd of speculators." ("Gold is Not an Investment," *New York Times*, May 23, 2011).

[36] www.alternet.org/economy/want-have-happy-planet-just-ask-costa-ricans-about-their-banks

Interest on a loan is never created with the principal of the loan and does not, even temporarily, increase the money supply, as the principal of the loan does, during the time the loan is outstanding. When the principal (also known as bank money, which is created *ex nihilo* [from nothing]) is paid off, the temporary increase in the money supply over the course of the loan is extinguished, resulting in a net gain/loss of zero, except for the interest, which must be pulled from the existent money supply to pay for the time during which the borrower used the private bank notes.[37]

Eventually, there is little or no money left in the money supply for labor, as it has all been extracted to pay interest to the usurers (capitalists), until the next round of lending is initiated, including lending to the government to spend monies (over and above the tax revenues and fees it collects) into the economy, so-called quantitative easing, which adds to the money supply and, in a private system, the national (i.e., the taxpayers') debt.

Further, as noted earlier, the moment that interest is charged on money, money becomes a commodity (capital)—that is, it changes from a unit of accounting for value into a store of value—with its value inflating geometrically and placed above the value of people, whose labor is— in that same instant that interest is charged—devalued and deflated geometrically (and which becomes a commodity: human capital). Essentially, this puts an abstraction that we have created (money in the form of capital) in control of our lives. In other words, *usury is the antithesis of labor*; it steals and destroys the value created by labor.

Such an inversion of the economic and spiritual value hierarchy posited by Lincoln, Franklin, and Aristotle—from labor being the focus to capital being the focus—has many ramifications, not the least of which

---

[37] The ultimate result of this dynamic, where the money supply shrinks via the collection of interest, is seen in three charts that form the core of our proof regarding optimal banking, currency, and credit practices, as shown and discussed in *Step 4—Making money a public utility through sustainable economics*.

is the debasing of human beings and their environment. Consider how premeditated scarcity, as practiced by contemporary financiers and their executive-class puppets, is used as a club to beat back better working conditions for labor or environmental protections: "Think of the economic consequences," they say. What could be plainer than to say that those who support such a value system have placed money—the almighty dollar, the golden calf, mammon, etc.—above all humanistic and spiritual values. Metaphorically speaking, this is doing the devil's work. Psychologically speaking, the root cause of this behavior is our shadow—our instincts and ego—tyrannizing our higher self.

Human behavior evolves through our own choices

Such a fear-based system necessarily defines human behavior as fixed—via the static concept of "human nature"—rather than seeing it in the context of constant universal change; that is, in consonance with the evolutionary forces that define the progression of light, from Singularity and the Big Bang to the infinite phenomena of the universe, within the course of which light becomes conscious of itself.

All of these considerations, from the economic to the spiritual, are why the story[38] of Jesus includes the incident in which he turns over the tables of the money changers and drives them from the Temple with a whip, declaring them "Thieves!" It is a perfect metaphor for the

---

[38] For the purposes of this point, it is irrelevant whether Jesus lived or whether he is a character in someone's book; in either case, these teachings have been brought into the world and it is to these spiritual teachings that we must measure up; just as, along the same lines, critic Harold Bloom asserts that "Shakespeare" invented the human, that is, a refinement of our awareness and behavior. In both cases, the evolutionary bar has been set high. So, let us not be sidetracked by any arguments that characterize any of our behavior as "human nature." There is no such thing. Everything is made from light, and light is constantly evolving. It may seem, in the blink-of-an-eye that is our life, that human behavior is unchanging, but in the long run, we have changed greatly and will continue to do so.

insidiousness of usury. Usury is the point at which economics and spirituality converge: usury puts things above people; sharing puts people above things.

Compound interest is a mathematical trick

Apologists for the present monetary sham have proposed a variety of mathematical scenarios which purport to show that interest is somehow created during what bankers call "the business cycle," but these constructs fall far short of proving anything other than how those well-versed in numbers can make them lie (as if $P + I = P$, when P and I are both > 0).[39] As we will see—in *Step 4—Making money a public utility through sustainable economics*—at the completion of the business cycle (within the paradigm of our current privately owned banking system), interest reduces the money supply, thus enabling the banks to control an ever-increasing proportion of assets, including corporations and governments. Clearly, private banking is not a business, but a tool of war, an assault on human dignity, and a means to world domination, as we shall detail in *Step 3—Transposing the money cartel's point-of-view*.

The process of compounding interest on principal is generally misunderstood because so many people have difficulty using and interpreting mathematical symbols. Our advice for those so challenged is to forget the self-serving and obfuscating formulas and apologies for the private creation of money and interest and look at the net effect of interest on the money supply[40] as well as the transfer of assets from the commonwealth, where these assets are created, to the balance sheets of those who control the world's central banks, currencies, and credit.[41]

---

[39] Where P = principal, and I = interest.

[40] Again, see our proof in *Step 4 – Making money a public utility through sustainable economics*.

[41] For details on how interest has become the single greatest cost across the entirety of the world economy, see Dr. Margrit Kennedy's presentation, "If Money

Just as the Occupy Wall Street movement insisted, and French economist Thomas Piketty recently proved,[42] the gap between those who create and those who steal is getting larger.

Should time be monetized?

Once interest has been applied, it enables the monetization of the time interval for which credit is extended by the usurer to the customer, institutionalizing the notion that "time equals money," as if such a limited, spiritually impoverished view of time provides a central truth around which life should be organized. Such a notion is also without scientific grounds, since it's clear, in our universe, we may deduce that the progression of space-time (excepting the anomalies at the lowest and highest vibrational and gravitational states)[43] is arithmetic, not geometric, even as space-time abides by Relativity.[44] Thus, the symbiosis between the intervals of space-time and value creation within its four-dimensional constraints has been recognized since antiquity:

> "Thou shalt not give him thy money upon interest, nor give him thy victuals for increase." —*Leviticus* 25:35-37[45]

Rules the World, Who Rules Money"
(http://www.margritkennedy.de/media/07262011_oslo-pres_ii-1_52.pdf) and her book, *Interest and Inflation-free Money*, (http://kennedy-bibliothek.info/data/bibo/media/GeldbuchEnglisch.pdf).

[42] *Capital in the Twenty-First Century*, The Belknap Press of Harvard University Press, Cambridge, MA, 2014.

[43] That is, absolute zero (or 0° Kelvin, i.e., the Bose-Einstein Condensate) and Singularity.

[44] That is, the speed of light remains constant (relatively speaking) throughout the universe, except at Singularity or 0° Kelvin.

[45] Usury, in the context of Judaism, Christianity, and Islam is discussed in *Step 2— Rejecting the false divisions of ethnicities, religions, political parties, and nationalities*.

On the other hand, it makes perfect sense that the money supply would, under ideal circumstances, be expanding and contracting at a rate in consonance with the addition or reduction of tradable value created by labor. *It is therefore labor's time which should be monetized and represent the creation of value*, not the duration for which capital, created from thin air, is loaned to labor, for the purpose of labor's diminishment.

Interest sleight-of-hand yields big results

Yet, we seem inured to interest, which is nothing more than a cheap trick, like the brain teaser we were taught as children: Would you rather have a million dollars, or a penny the first day, doubled every day for a month? The neophyte takes the million dollars, turning down $5,368,709.12.

> "Once a nation parts with the control of its currency and credit, it matters not who makes that nation's laws. Usury, once in control, will wreck any nation. Until the control of the issue of currency and credit is restored to government and recognized as its most conspicuous and sacred responsibility, all talk of the sovereignty of Parliament and of democracy is idle and futile."
> —William Lyon Mackenzie King, Canadian Prime Minister, 1935[46]

Corporate and personal debt are the usurers' means to power

Mortgages are an extension of the trick of interest, wherein interest is charged up front, so that while money-lenders compound interest over the life of the loan, say 30 years, they have front-loaded the interest payment, charging for time that has not yet occurred. Adding insult to

---

[46] This excerpt from a speech by King appeared in an article by Louis Even, first published in the March 1, 1958 issue of the *Vers Demain Journal*.

injury, by the addition of this inverted schedule of amortization, the lien holders retain a greater percentage of the asset. This is particularly handy for the usurers, since they also determine the periodic contractions of the money supply (i.e., depressions that are achieved through manipulation of events and markets) by which they seize collateralized assets (our homes and other fruits of our labor) at fire sale prices.

Compound interest compounded by fraud

Finally, there is the matter of collusion, fraud, and racketeering in the setting of interest rates, as became clear in July 2012 with the LIBOR scandal, involving financial instruments from A to Z, including the suppression of interest rates to keep the derivatives markets from collapsing the global financial house of cards.[47] This manipulation of worldwide interest rates has been dubbed "the crime of the century,"[48] but that's an understatement.[49] Such criminal machinations put private banks in the odd position of holding down interest rates to keep the system going,[50] which explains why they are spending their money on manipulating and speculating in high-return markets, rather than loaning money to the medium and small-sized businesses that represented half the jobs in the U.S. before the 2008 crash that they, the cartel, manufactured.

---

[47] http://truth-out.org/news/item/9876-the-jpmorgan-derivatives-propping-up-us-debt-why-the-senate-wont-touch-jamie-dimon

[48] http://www.truthdig.com/report/item/crime_of_the_century_20120706/; http://www.washingtonpost.com/blogs/ezra-klein/wp/2012/07/05/explainer-why-the-libor-scandal-is-a-bigger-deal-than-jpmorgan/; and http://marketday.nbcnews.com/_news/2012/07/11/12684779-a-scandal-over-rate-fixing-is-about-to-hit-the-us

[49] We say this despite the fact that none of the bankers responsible for this fraud were prosecuted. http://www.nytimes.com/2015/05/21/business/dealbook/5-big-banks-to-pay-billions-and-plead-guilty-in-currency-and-interest-rate-cases.html

[50] http://www.munknee.com/will-collapse-the-entire-u-s-financial-system/

Yet, while the rigging of LIBOR[51] may have slowed down the usury cycle (earlier it was used to speed it up), it also supported a more lucrative scam that was initiated before the interest rate plunge: manipulating the municipal bond market[52] and selling interest rate swaps to cities (such as Baltimore,[53] Oakland,[54] and Philadelphia,[55] which sued), counties, states, and other taxing districts (e.g., public schools), as well as pension funds, with the expressed consent and obeisance of the government functionaries necessary to create the contract.[56]

Every level of the financial system is rigged,[57] including:

- The incestuous relationship between the Fed and the so-called

---

[51] http://dealbook.nytimes.com/2012/06/27/barclays-said-to-settle-regulatory-claims-over-benchmark-manipulation; http://www.telegraph.co.uk/finance/newsbysector/banksandfinance/9368430/Libor-scandal-How-I-manipulated-the-bank-borrowing-rate.html; http://www.examiner.com/video/experts-explain-libor-profit-rigging; and http://www.rollingstone.com/politics/blogs/taibblog/libor-banking-scandal-deepens-barclays-releases-damning-email-implicates-british-government-20120704

[52] http://www.rollingstone.com/politics/news/the-scam-wall-street-learned-from-the-mafia-20120620#ixzz1yS3rPeCP

[53] http://www.baltimoresun.com/news/opinion/editorial/bs-ed-libor-20120716-story.html

[54] http://www.forbes.com/sites/halahtouryalai/2012/07/11/city-of-oakland-taps-occupy-wall-street-to-take-on-goldman-sachs/

[55] http://www.forbes.com/sites/halahtouryalai/2012/07/11/city-of-oakland-taps-occupy-wall-street-to-take-on-goldman-sachs/

[56] http://readersupportednews.org/off-site-opinion-section/72-72/12267-british-government-implicated-in-libor-banking-scandal Another example, closer to home, is that of Michael Bennet who, as head of the Denver Public Schools, purchased these tricked-up instruments, which then saddled the district with a massive debt. As an unspoken reward, Bennet became a U.S. Senator.

[57] http://www.washingtonsblog.com/2012/07/libor-is-not-the-only-manipulated-economic-indicator.html

"too big to fail" (TBTF) banks that own it, for whom the Fed guarantees any losses resulting from premeditated and repeated speculative excesses;

- The Fed's Permanent Open Market Operations purchases of U.S. Treasury bonds[58] through so-called "market makers," i.e., the TBTF banks[59];

- The Fed's actions disguised as foreign purchases,[60] all of which fund computerized front running[61] in the stock market, where superfast programs skirt the rules to drive prices up and down[62] and where insider trading is rampant; and, finally,

- The banking regulations set by the financiers through their proxies, the central banks and the Bank of International Settlements (BIS), used to attack target organizations, including nation-states and independent banks.[63]

Whenever the cartel's criminal activities become public knowledge, the pro forma strategy of so-called regulators is to pretend to investigate[64]

---

[58] http://www.opednews.com/articles/THE-U-S-STOCK-MARKET-IS-R-by-lila-york-101227-303.html

[59] http://www.opednews.com/articles/The-Real-Libor-Scandal-by-Paul-Craig-Roberts-120714-763.html

[60] http://georgewashington2.blogspot.com/2009/09/is-treasury-faking-foreign-purchases-of.html and https://usawatchdog.com/fed-laundering-treasury-purchases-in-belgium-to-disguise-whats-happening-paul-craig-roberts/

[61] http://www.webofdebt.com/articles/computerized_front_running.php

[62] http://savethefloor.com/savethefloor/is-the-stock-market-rigged-excerpt/; and http://www.alternet.org/story/148008/unreal%3A_banks%27_created_fake_dem and_to_boost_profits_and_yearly_bonuses

[63] For example, when the BIS changed reserve requirements to burst Japan's "real estate bubble" in the late '90's. Much of the squeeze on independent banks is a result of similar pressures and, to a degree, accounts for the high rate of independent bank failures and takeovers, except in North Dakota, where the state-owned Bank of North Dakota (BND) provides help to local banks. (More on the BND in *Step 4—Making money a public utility through sustainable economics*.)

[64] http://www.guardian.co.uk/business/2012/jul/13/libor-scandal-banking-inquiry-

the transgressions, consolidate any lawsuits (so that a small group of people can be controlled, much like they did in corralling the 50 states attorneys general to defuse the MERS scandal[65]), slap a few hands, and then repeat this approach for the next round of criminal activities. When the banks, the Fed, and the regulators all work hand-in-hand,[66] the heads of the crime families go scot free.[67]

Money-as-a-commodity lent with interest creates the "business cycle"

Despite the criminal framework of the system, on the basis of a loan agreement drawn up by private lenders, compounded interest is expected to be created magically and paid back from the existing money supply. Obviously, such a debt-based, interest-bearing system creates a shortage of money, unless the system is constantly expanding with new debt, which it is not; rather, the money supply expands and contracts in response to what the private banks call "the business cycle."

---

whitewash

[65] http://www.huffingtonpost.com/2012/01/12/attorney-general-foreclosure-settlement-eric-schneiderman-beau-biden_n_1202643.html; Also, *More Settlement Reactions: The Sunday Times* included a pair of editorials on the $25 billion pact announced last week between the mortgage mega-servicers and federal and state regulators. The first piece calls the foreclosure robo-signing settlement "a wrist slap compared with the economic damage wrought by the banks in the housing bubble and bust."
https://www.americanbanker.com/morning-scan/monday-february-13
[66] http://www.huffingtonpost.com/2012/07/16/tim-geithner-libor_n_1674552.html; and http://www.huffingtonpost.com/2012/07/13/new-york-fed-libor-documents_n_1671524.html, as well as http://www.reuters.com/article/2012/01/20/us-usa-holder-mortgage-idUSTRE80J0PH20120120
[67] http://dealbook.nytimes.com/2012/08/09/goldman-says-sec-has-ended-mortgage-investigation/

When the economy is expanding, this drain (interest being removed from the money supply) goes relatively unnoticed,[68] despite the fact that the interest owed continues to accumulate, because the private banks choose to either recirculate their interest income (by applying it to their reserves and lending against that), thus expanding their loan exposure, or by issuing dividends, or simply by borrowing reserves from the Fed and creating more temporary bank money; but, when the banks choose to contract the money supply, all of that interest comes due, which means that money is taken out of circulation and withheld, accelerating the contraction, since loans are being paid off or defaulted upon and few new loans are being made.

So, at the end of the so-called "business cycle," the casino chips begin to disappear and the house rakes in the collateral, while the little people suffer induced bankruptcies, foreclosures, and joblessness. The net result: severe devaluation to the commonwealth, whose money supply otherwise would never contract (except, possibly, as a result of "acts of G-d," or declining population or value reduction); that is, with public control over money creation, the money supply would remain proportional to the goods and services in circulation.[69]

In other words, in a privately controlled banking system, commercial bank loans and credit cards are nothing more than bait, and interest is the poison pill: the greater the economy, the greater the money supply; the greater the money supply, the greater the interest-generated debt— until the loans are called.

> "... the truth is, that capital may be produced by industry, and accumulated by economy; but jugglers only will propose to

---

[68] After the 2008 manufactured crash, the banks re-inflated the currency: Central Banks Act With a New Boldness www.nytimes.com/2013/05/29/business/central-banks-act-with-a-new-boldness.html

[69] We'll look at the details of the problem of interest, in the context of public versus private banking, in *Step 4—Making money a public utility through sustainable economics.*

create it by legerdemain tricks with paper." —Thomas Jefferson, in a letter to John W. Eppes, 1813

In fact, the financiers—through their public relations department mouthpiece, *The New York Times*—freely argue that the manipulated instability of markets, which results from the false value (interest) that they add at every turn, is preferable to sustainability.[70] What the money changers are saying is that their objective is theft; and, in fact, as scandal after scandal shows, **fraud is their business model**. More on that in *Step 3—Transposing the money cartel's point-of-view*.

Going back to our original question in this section—"What happens when money-as-an-accounting gets confused with money-as-a-commodity?"—we see that when money is mistakenly used as a commodity, rather than as a unit of account, we end up with a system that values capital over labor, material objects over people, and the devil's work over our God-given gifts (or, in psychological terms, our shadow [instincts and ego] over our higher self).

> "And the devil, taking him up into a high mountain, shewed unto him all the kingdoms of the world in a moment of time. And the devil said unto him, all this power will I give thee, and the glory of them: for that is delivered unto me; and to whomsoever I will, I give it. If thou therefore wilt worship me, all shall be thine. And Jesus answered and said unto him, Get thee behind me, Satan ..." —*Luke* 4:5-8

Private ownership of money begets debt slavery

When money ceases to be used for creating and distributing what is needed for society—food, clothing, shelter, education, healthcare, culture, etc.—and begins to be used for the pursuit of making more money, the market becomes subject to political and economic forces

---

[70] http://www.nytimes.com/2012/11/03/opinion/forget-sustainability-its-about-resilience.html

directed by those who accumulate and leverage their profit to create more profit ("money making money"), a vicious cycle that subjects the vast majority of people to a form of slavery in which most people never have enough money to meet their basic needs.

This is because money has been taken out of the system to: pay for interest; meet arbitrary reserve requirements required by privately controlled central banks; create dividends for shareholders; or, simply to create a shortage of money to precipitate bankruptcies, foreclosures, and joblessness, which, in turn, facilitate the theft of collateralized assets.

In such a system, money becomes an end in itself, and those who profit by its manipulation create a permanent inflationary and deflationary cycle, where there is alternately too much money and then not enough. For example, since 1890 there have been 25 recessions and depressions. These ups and downs (the so-called "business cycle") are simply a means of funding the creation of assets and then usurping them.

Those who control the money supply believe that these assets are rightly theirs (as the notorious financier, Andrew Mellon, once said: "In a depression, assets return to their rightful owner."), since they funded the assets through loans and other debt instruments based on the private bank notes (the money supply) that they own. They use this tautology, loans based on the creation and lending of money that they never possessed in the first place, to assert their right to control the public money supply, as if "legal tender" was a commodity to be franchised like McDonald's hamburgers. Going back to the goldsmiths, whose profits from lending—based on their clients' assets and, in some case, non-existent "reserves"—bought them the licenses to continue their counterfeiting protected by "law": This is now the practice we call "banking."

The net result is that the financiers end up with an ever-increasing percentage of the assets, as detailed in a recent study by the Swiss

Federal Institute of Technology in Zurich.[71] Currently, no more than 147 organizations (publicly held banks and holding companies) control the core of the global economy.[72] This is easily accomplished through private control of the money creation process and charging the world interest for the use of private bank notes that supplanted sovereign currency as legal tender.

For example, consider that, in the same year of the Swiss study, of the 50 largest U.S. corporations, 80% of the cash was in the hands of four banks: Goldman Sachs, JPMorgan Chase, Citigroup, and Bank of America.[73] As Reuters reported, this does not include the approximately $32 trillion that private parties have looted and stashed in offshore "tax havens,"[74] that is, pirate treasure buried on tropical islands.

The pirates have taken over the governments: private banks are not businesses, in the sense that labor creates goods or services; they are a means of using money to acquire assets and power; they are political organizations with the most regressive of objectives, that is, corporate control over the state—one of the textbook definitions of fascism.[75]

Interest: Borrowing exponentially from the future

---

[71] Stefania Vitali, James B. Glattfelder, and Stefano Battiston, *The network of global corporate control*, ETH Zurich, 2011.

[72] We can only speculate on the structure above these 147 organizations, which are, in turn, controlled by closely-held and privately-held holding companies, but based on a close examination of the "too big to fail" banks and their nexus of connections in this structure, the number is certainly less than 20.

[73] http://www.opednews.com/articles/Call-me-crazy-but-I-like-by-Henry-Porter-101202-267.html

[74] http://news.yahoo.com/super-rich-hold-32-trillion-offshore-havens-090225488--sector.html

[75] George H. Sabine, *A History of Political Theory*, 3rd Edition, Holt, Rinehart and Winston, New York, 1961, p. 919.

The question then arises as to the necessity of interest, particularly in the implementation of a sustainable model. Like Macbeth's urge to "... jump the life to come,"[76] interest invokes labor that was not and will never be performed, claiming, essentially, that their private currency somehow increases in value (at a compounded rate, no less!), despite creating it from thin air.

This brings us back to humanistic and spiritual values. Under the current paradigm of usury and debt slavery, there is an expectation of return on capital just as we would expect for the use of our labor or any resource. Such a perspective is perfectly consistent with the capitalist paradigm, within which everything is commodified; however, as we examine the nature of money, what we discover is that it is not a commodity, like gold or silver, nor is it a service, like labor—it is a relationship and an agreement involving both labor and commodities that facilitates their exchange.

> "So everything should have its value: that makes possible exchange and a common market. Money makes all things commensurable. Without exchange no community, without equality no exchange, without commensurability no equality."
> —Aristotle, *Nicomachean Ethics*

As Aristotle indicates, we have a choice in the role that money plays when we assign value. We can put human beings (labor) front and center in our system, or we can have our existence ruled by abstractions (money) and commodities (gold, silver, oil, diamonds, etc.).

If we wish to create an economy in which human beings are valued over things, then money is simply a means of accounting for our accumulated labor. It is not something that is loaned between people with the intent of being compounded, since it has no existence outside of accounting for our labor. Again, interest is the antithesis of labor, since it reduces the value created by labor via the contraction of the

---

[76] "William Shake-speare," *Macbeth*, I, vii, 7.

money supply to satisfy its "legal" demand.

The problem of agit-prop

As more and more people begin to catch-on to the fraudulent practices underlying our monetary and financial systems—overcoming the financiers' concerted effort to have us confuse money with commodities and thereby persuade citizens to act against their own interests—and as more and more people see how the cartel's power over money creation has enabled this small group to control almost all the key corporate and formerly sovereign resources on the planet, the money cartel has stepped up its propaganda efforts to obfuscate the situation.

This effort isn't confined to the mass and social media, which has been consolidated into a handful of corporations, but across the entire fabric of society, from the commercial to the spiritual and everything in-between, including education, politics, food, housing, sports, religion, and culture. The pervasiveness of the cartel's behavior-modification techniques has established a baseline point-of-view for significant segments of society; yet, this seemingly monolithic control masks significant skepticism among those living under its matrix. The cartel's heavy-handed suppression of large-scale protests when their news blackouts fail, as happened with Occupy Wall Street, tells us both the seriousness of their perpetrations and their growing fear of the evolution of mass consciousness. Clearly, the self-described "New World Order's"[77] view of society's prospects and of "human nature" is dystopian. It's the only way they can justify their totalitarian behavior.

All successful organizations that propose an alternate path, including spontaneous movements and clever marketplace attractions, are swallowed up by a juggernaut of corporate and government agents marching to the tune of the usurer-kings and their black ops. In the

---

[77] A term popularized by George H.W. Bush and David Rockefeller.

political sphere, for instance, Trump supporters and other associated extremists are herded by their puppet masters through media gauntlets warning of impending economic and political doom—but these "minutemen" have missed the boat: the overthrow of "the American way of life" (the usurpation of democracy and laissez-faire capitalism) that they feared has long since passed, with only a few well-placed bullets needed to facilitate the coup d'état. Tea Party darlings, such as Ron or Rand Paul or Paul Ryan, appeal to distrust of big government to deflect the focus from the corporate takeover of the state, beating the drum, for instance, to "End the Fed" and replace it with the gold standard,[78] as if those who control the Fed were somehow separate from those who have cornered the gold market. The Tea Party and its sequel movements are nothing more than a creation of the cartel, via Big Tobacco and other oligarchies.[79]

Meanwhile, so-called liberalism, and even the Occupy phenomenon, are corralled by similar tactics—infiltration aimed at undermining their movements through violence—or, rendering them ineffective by employing the federalized the police and *agent provocateurs* to deny them their right to peacefully assemble. Finally, the left is manipulated by cartel apologists, such as Bill Maher, who mocked Occupy Wall Street's resilient decentralized model and suggested that they create a formal organization; in other words, so they can be hijacked.[80] The

---

[78] As Texas will apparently attempt to do: http://www.zerohedge.com/news/2016-05-17/texas-begins-construction-gold-depository

[79] http://www.opednews.com/Quicklink/Study-Confirms-Tea-Party-W-in-General_News-130211-15.html

[80] http://www.huffingtonpost.com/2012/06/09/bill-maher-mocks-occupy-wall-street_n_1583616.html. On the surface, it seems funny and reasonable, but what Maher is suggesting is exactly what the New World Order (NWO) wants—to break up the movement, which they did by federalizing local police forces through the Department of Homeland Security and through direct contributions (to the NYPD by JPMorgan Chase), and then by forcing the movement into electoral politics, to form organizations that can then be infiltrated and sabotaged. Here's an example of this strategy, baiting Muslims to become terrorists:

same tactics have been exported worldwide, for example, in Ukraine.[81]

The banks have used such tactics for at least 500 years in Europe, long before England's North American colonies became a nation. Thereafter, the American Revolution was continually sold out— beginning with charters for the First and Second Bank of the U.S. (controlled by the privately owned Bank of England) and continuing until the bankers' treasonous efforts were finally formalized in the Federal Reserve Act—bringing us 19 recessions since that fateful day, December 23, 1913, when much of Congress was on recess. Endless convoluted arguments have been invented to justify this wholesale sellout of our sovereign republic.

Religion fuels corporate hegemony as well, as contemporary pulpits are filled with snake oil salesmen hawking the notion that "rendering unto Caesar" is, literally, what Jesus suggested, rather than as an expression underscoring his contempt for the crass materialism of Rome. As we shall discover in the next chapter, this corporate interpretation of Christianity does not jibe with historical facts; rather, it is agit-prop designed to legitimize the financiers' role in controlling the planet.

How do we change the equation and use money to improve our lives?

Clearly, if we are going to master money and use it to benefit humanity, we must face the fact that a debt-based, interest-bearing system, as a matter of course, cyclically creates a shortage of money—thereby systematically denying us the currency needed to maintain our assets— while, simultaneously, permitting the largest, "too big to fail" banks that own the money supply, to subsidize their losses—by advancing

---

http://www.huffingtonpost.com/2012/10/23/shamiur-rahman-nypd-paid-muslims-bait-jihad-terrorism_n_2005141.html.

[81] http://www.nytimes.com/2013/12/23/world/europe/ukraine-movement-strong-on-solidarity-struggles-for-a-plan.html

themselves unlimited funds (through TARP, quantitative easing, and other cleverly named bail-out shams)—and use those taxpayer-supported subsidies to seize the hard-earned fruits of our labor for pennies on the dollar.

To correct these criminal practices, our objective must be to create a system that is able to grow without the burden of an ever-increasing debt that comes from private bankers taxing our money supply via compound interest.

To do so requires that our currency, credit, and money supply be created and managed in the public interest. Such a system is called public banking (the efficacy of which we detail in *Step 4—Making money a public utility through sustainable economics*). In sum, we must transform the current practice of debt-based slavery into a practice of credit-based freedom.

By credit-based freedom we mean humanity credits in a publicly controlled monetary system where—as labor is replaced by machines, computers, robots, and artificial intelligence—universal income, healthcare, and education are the norm. In an advanced privately controlled monetary system, as labor is digitalized, the unemployed labor force is seen as "useless eaters"; or, as Dickens' Scrooge (a usurer in the City of London) suggests: "If they (the poor) would rather die, they had better do it, and decrease the surplus population." Thus, the aspirations of humankind, to have more time for creative endeavors, will only happen in a publicly controlled monetary system.

Such a transformation depends upon a qualitative change in consciousness—conscious spiritual evolution—that is, overcoming the forces and ideas that limit human potential, including the destruction of language and thought, as Orwell foretold.

STEP 2—REJECTING THE FALSE DIVISIONS OF ETHNICITIES, RELIGIONS, POLITICAL PARTIES, AND NATIONALITIES

If thought corrupts language, language can also corrupt thought. —George Orwell, Politics and the English Language, *1946*

The fact that the vast majority of the population accepts, and is made to accept, this society, does not render it less irrational and less reprehensible. The distinction between true and false consciousness, real and immediate interest, still is meaningful. —Herbert Marcuse, One-Dimensional Man, *1964*

The inversion of humanistic value

As we saw in the previous chapter, humanistic values have been supplanted by the exigencies of capital, which is the value of labor that has been converted into a commodity by charging interest for its use. To support this inversion, the central bankers, whose financial resources are bottomless, have purchased and developed a sophisticated matrix of scientific, educational, journalistic, political, economic, medical, and religious rationalizations—all serving to support this inversion of value.

One of the techniques of successful propaganda is to repeat a statement over and over again until people believe it to be true, as contemporary intercourse with any of the aforementioned corrupted academic and commercial disciplines amply demonstrates. This is usually accomplished via a technique called "limited hangout" in the world of intelligence services, meaning using known truths to promulgate misdirection and lies.

So, to transform the world into a sustainable and progressive place, we must reverse-engineer contemporary thought paradigms and deconstruct the underlying deceit disseminated via the banking pyramid's ubiquitous disinformation machine, whose mission it is to justify the cartel's criminal business model and stranglehold on the globe.

> "Ignorance is Strength
> Freedom is Slavery
> War is Peace." —George Orwell, *1984*

The convergence of science and spirituality

Truly, the web of misdirection woven by the usurers and their ideologues is seductive, preying on instincts that we, as a species, have not yet succeeded in tempering to serve our evolutionary needs. As noted in our Introduction, we are on the cusp between two evolutionary stages in human development—moving from mastering symbolic forms (language, music, mathematics, etc.), that is, "subconscious mental evolution," to the overcoming of the tyranny of the instincts and the ego, i.e., "conscious spiritual evolution."

The framework for the convergence of science and spirituality, as set forth in Solomon's Proof, indicates that the human attainment of mastery of symbolic forms, however limited the audience may be at this time, is an achievement that catapults us beyond the limited mathematical confines of theoretical physics' "final theory" to a broader framework inclusive of all aspects of our universe, enabling our transition as a species into a new paradigm of human development, where we can see the holistic truth embedded in a myriad of once-disparate points-of-view. Yet, both scientific and spiritual "leadership," with few exceptions, resist this reconciliation, each of these barricaded mindsets insisting on its own exclusive and limited conclusions.

Roadblocks to accepting the implications Relativity and Singularity

Einstein faced similar roadblocks when he first presented Relativity to the German physics establishment. As noted in a review of Steven Gimbel's *Einstein's Jewish Science*, "It's no wonder Nazis hated relativity. They lived in a world of absolutes."[82] Gimbel argues that, even though Einstein was not particularly religious, he was well-versed in Talmudic logic, which accepts that "there is an absolute truth, but this truth is not directly and completely available to us." Gimbel then explains, "It turns out that exactly the same style of thinking occurs in the relativity theory and in some of Einstein's other research."

So, while the widespread acceptance of Solomon's Proof—including the implications of the Singularity (the 1st dimension) in space-time— may be temporarily suppressed by an increasingly aggressive and, yet, increasingly irrelevant corporate science bloc, which views the world through the narrow lens of causal reasoning (and investor satisfaction), we shall follow a broader logical paradigm, including acausal reasoning, intrinsic to Einstein's Theory of Relativity ("Light is both a wave and a particle at the same time."), as well as Werner Heisenberg's Uncertainty Principle ("If you look for the wave, you see the wave; if you look for the particle, you see the particle.").

The Protestant Ethic and the Spirit of Capitalism

Given the increasing gap between rich and poor, the sharp spike in religious fundamentalism, and the impunity with which corporate-

---

[82] George Johnson, "Quantum Leaps," *New York Times*, August 3, 2012. http://www.nytimes.com/2012/08/05/books/review/einsteins-jewish-science-by-steven-gimbel.html

controlled states seize resources to which they have no legitimate claim, one of our first priorities in unravelling the conflation of unrelated terms—while reverse-engineering the epidemic of corporate Newspeak[83]—must be to disable the use of religious dogma to justify greed and war.

Since surveys indicate that three-quarters of Americans (those who live within the influence of world's most powerful financial and military apparatus) consider themselves to be Christians, let's begin there.[84]

It has become a tenet of faith for many Christians that they can simultaneously practice their religion and conduct economic affairs in their own self-interest. Indeed, ever since the Protestant Reformation arose from the pressures of the Industrial Revolution, the pulpits of Christianity have been used to turn wealth (economic success) into an indication of favor from G-d.[85]

Let's go back to the source of Christianity and see if such thinking holds up.

> "I say unto you, it is easier for a camel to go through the eye of a needle, than for a rich man to enter into the kingdom of God."
> —*Matthew* 19:24

---

[83] In Orwell's *1984*, the name given to English after it had been destroyed by the Party.

[84] Barry A. Kosmin and Ariela Keysar (2009). "AMERICAN RELIGIOUS IDENTIFICATION SURVEY (ARIS) 2008" (PDF). Hartford, Connecticut, USA: Trinity College. http://b27.cc.trincoll.edu/weblogs/AmericanReligionSurvey-ARIS/reports/ARIS_Report_2008.pdf. Retrieved 2009-04-01.

[85] See Max Weber, *The Protestant Ethic and the Spirit of Capitalism—the relationships between religion and the economic and social life in modern culture*, translated by Talcott Parsons, with a Foreword by R.H. Tawney, Charles Scribner's sons, New York, 1958, and R.H. Tawney, *Religion and the Rise of Capitalism—A historical study*, New American Library, New York, 1954.

Jesus walked a tightrope regarding money

There are, of course, a variety of quotes in the Christian Bible, some of which we have already cited, that are obviously consistent with the above, with one pre-eminent enigmatic exception:

> "Render therefore unto Caesar the things which are Caesar's; and unto God the things that are God's." —*Matthew* 22:21; *Mark* 12:17; *Luke* 20:25

Following up from the previous chapter, where we promised to show how the interpretation of this famous phrase has been completely reversed from its historical context, we note that, as Michael Baigent so astutely documents in *The Jesus Papers: Exposing the Greatest Cover-Up in History*,[86] Jesus' remarks were carefully couched to respond to a trick question on the part of the Pharisees. Cognizant of the slaughter the Romans had inflicted on Jews who refused to pay taxes to the state, Jesus was seeking to avoid a confrontation over this particular issue. Orthodox fundamentalists may have thought they were tricking Jesus into choosing between supporting Rome (and therefore its taxation) and supporting the indigenous uprising of Judea, but Jesus' response was a trick as well.

Showing consistency with his earlier remarks that "You cannot serve God and Mammon," he tells the Pharisees to take the coin with Caesar's image and give it back to Caesar, since, as shown by his actions against the moneychangers in the Temple, Jesus rejects a medium of exchange based on usury.[87] In such a response, Jesus shows

---

[86] HarperSanFrancisco, 2006.

[87] "If you have money, do not lend it at interest, but give it to one from whom you will not get it back." --*The Gospel of Thomas* (95). *The Gospel of Thomas* and other texts found at Nag Hammadi [*Gnostic Gospels*] and Qumran [*Dead Sea Scrolls*] predate the texts that were edited and synthesized by Bishop Irenaeus of Lyon [3rd Century CE] and the Council of Nicaea [4th Century CE] to form what is currently

his contempt for the empire, while avoiding incarceration and torture over this point. He had bigger fish to fry. It's worth noting that the Roman Senate at this time was populated entirely by usurers, whose practices resulted in a major financial crisis in 33 CE.[88]

Rome shifted the blame for Jesus' death to the Jews

In support of the notion of Jesus as a political as well as spiritual figure, Baigent perceptively points out that Jesus was crucified, a Roman punishment for sedition, not stoned, as he would have been if it were the Jews who caused him to be executed for religious crimes. From this key fabrication—i.e., that the Jews ordered Jesus' crucifixion, cemented into the so-called *New Testament* under Constantine in 325 C.E.—comes the source of Anti-Semitism in Christianity that leads directly to Mohammed's purges, the Spanish Inquisition, the Russian pogroms, and the German "final solution."

So, it is no coincidence that the Roman Catholic Church aligned itself with the Nazis. Both parties had a stake in making sure that Jesus, or a Jewish prophet like him, would never appear again. The Muslims were on board with this as well. They had their own SS brigade (Handzar), personally reviewed by Hitler and the Mufti of Jerusalem, to contribute to the extermination of the Jews. Jews remain fair game for Muslims

---

used as the Christian Bible. As this particular passage from Thomas shows, the unedited text reveals important points that have been suppressed.

[88] *Observations on: I. The Answer of M L'Abbé de Vertot to the late Earl Stanhope's Inquiry concerning the Senate of Ancient Rome, dated December 1719; II. A Dissertation upon the Constitution of the Roman Senate, by a Gentleman, published in 1743; III. A Treatise on the Roman Senate, by Dr. Conyers Middleton, published in 1747; IV. An Essay on the Roman Senate, by Dr. Thomas Chapman, published in 1750; by Mr. Hooke, published in 1758,* specifically "Observations of Dr. Middleton's Treatise and Dr. Chapman's Essay on the Roman Senate," p. 189.

throughout Europe[89] and in the Levant,[90] as well as for many Christians, based on their belief in the anti-Semitic propaganda of the Christian Bible.

The churches worship materialism

For Christian churches to twist the meaning of "Render therefore unto Caesar the things which are Caesar's; and unto God the things that are God's" into a justification for the enslavement of believers to the cynical earthly powers of Mammon is the ultimate inversion of how Jesus acted and taught.

No wonder then, that a religion such as Christianity—which has been hijacked by the financial powers—supports wars, torture, and other crimes against humanity, as it tacitly does by using the pulpit to endorse the corporate shills who fill the halls of Congress and governments everywhere. Add this to the sex crimes that churches have committed and suppressed for centuries and we see the depths to which these institutions—which present themselves as disciples of Jesus—have plunged. They had better pray for their own spiritual resurrection, because they have crossed the river Styx into Hades and sold their souls to the Plutocracy.[91]

---

[89] http://www.thelocal.fr/20160531/french-jews-flee-paris-suburbs-over-rising-anti-semitism and http://www.nrg.co.il/online/1/ART2/676/485.html

[90] https://www.israelislamandendtimes.com/palestinian-authority-paid-terrorists-nearly-350-million-2017/, http://www.jpost.com/Magazine/Murdering-Jewish-children-is-for-Allah-according-to-the-Palestinian-Authority-411334, https://www.washingtonpost.com/opinions/mr-zarifs-holocaust-denial-denial/2016/05/09/2b5570b6-160a-11e6-9e16-2e5a123aac62_story.html, and https://www.memri.org/tv/jordan-media-director-protocols-elders-zion-abhorred-treacherous-jews/transcript

[91] We say this regardless of the present pope's (Francis') message. He is the titular head of some of the wealthiest institutions on the planet—i.e., the Church and the Vatican Bank—and yet we see no indication that any substantial amounts of these assets have been used to back up Francis' appeals to help the poor. Additionally, the creation of a tribunal to oversee its clergy's sex crimes has made a couple of

To this behavior that we witness from so-called Christians, Jesus would say,

> "Depart from me, you who are cursed, into the eternal fire prepared for the devil and his angels. For I was hungry and you gave me nothing to eat, I was thirsty and you gave me nothing to drink, I was a stranger and you did not invite me in, I needed clothes and you did not clothe me, I was sick and in prison and you did not look after me." They also will answer, "Lord, when did we see you hungry or thirsty or a stranger or needing clothes or sick or in prison, and did not help you?" He will reply, "I tell you the truth, whatever you did not do for one of the least among you, you did not do for me." —*Matthew* 25:41-45

Here again, I would ask you to put aside any negativity you may rightfully or wrongfully hold against any religion, or Christianity in particular, and simply consider that someone said or wrote the above quotation, which stands on its own as spiritual advice.

Religions and the Empire are one

For obvious reasons, most modern churches work very hard to maintain the illusion of separation between economic and spiritual behavior, using "Render therefore unto Caesar the things which are Caesar's; and unto God the things that are God's" as a partition to maintain their

---

examples (http://www.usnews.com/news/world/articles/2015/06/15/us-archbishop-resigns-after-archdiocese-charged-with-coverup), while still protecting other criminals (http://indiancountrytodaymedianetwork.com/2014/08/28/why-pope-francis-protecting-high-ranking-pedophile-156630, including the previous pope (http://www.huffingtonpost.com/2013/02/17/pope-immunity_n_2708518.html). Also, http://www.dw.com/en/australia-reveals-over-4000-alleged-incidents-of-abuse-by-catholic-priests/a-37424453

psychopathology. But the actual teachings argue for a frank discussion. The Torah and the Christian Bible mention money and financial matters—including gold, silver, wealth, riches, inheritance, debt, and poverty—more than nearly any other subject. So, why the confusion over the message in today's so-called religions?

As it turns out, both prophets and social theorists predicted this: humankind would come to worship golden idols and, as a result, everything, including humans, would become commodified; that is, political economy and prophesy have now converged:

> "Then [Jesus] said to them, 'Watch out! Be on your guard against all kinds of greed; a man's life does not consist in the abundance of his possessions.'" (*Luke* 12:15)

> "On the basis of political economy itself … we have shown that the worker sinks to the level of a commodity and becomes indeed the most wretched of commodities …" Karl Marx, *Economic and Philosophical Manuscripts of 1844.*

Bankers worship the Golden Calf

There is no better source for examples of how greed poisons human relationships than the banking industry, which, like Charles Dickens' Ebenezer Scrooge, aims to kill off "the surplus population." Dickens makes it very clear in *A Christmas Carol* that, in the beginning, Scrooge is no Christian. Just so, those who operate the private banks that control a majority of the world's economies are not Jews, or Christians, or Muslims, etc. They worship a golden idol, just as Scrooge's one-time fiancée, Belle, said of him.

Such idolatry allows them to perform criminal acts ("Just business, you understand," they say) and characterize it in socially acceptable terms (the very definition of psychopathology); for example: to conjure money from nothing and extend it as credit, as if they had the sovereign power to create currency, and then charge interest on this faux currency (what we call "Federal" Reserve Notes).

The currency created by these illegitimate agents is used to drive a wedge between people, rather than unite them. That is why Jesus rejected the coin with Caesar's image on it, why Moses demolished the golden calf, and why the Qur'an forbids usury. Usury is a weapon for the theft of labor; that is, it robs individuals of the value they create via their labor.

In religious terms, worship of the golden calf is a direct manifestation of greed, a deadly sin; in other words, worship of the golden calf is the disease of materialism, which is, ultimately, a disease of the spirit. Thus, as we noted in our Introduction, global transformation requires both economic and spiritual solutions.

Rejecting the conflation of religion and political economy

Yet, while Judaism, Christianity, and Islam do not support usury, one would not know it by the behavior of those nations associated with these religious persuasions; rather, these states act as proxies for the financiers.

For example, the United States, United Kingdom, France, Saudi Arabia, and Israel are represented as sovereign nations operating under the influence of principles found in Christianity, Islam, and Judaism, which are supposedly practiced by the majority of their citizens; but, based on the belligerent policies of these governments—as public-sector subsidiaries of the Anglo-Euro-American banking cartel—in Afghanistan, Iraq, Libya, Syria, Yemen, and Gaza, no one could seriously argue that those who control the governments of these countries could be practitioners of any religion or follow any spiritual practice.[92]

Instead, those who attempt to actually follow the teachings of their scriptures are considered cannon fodder, either as soldiers or victims, to those who control these former nation-states.[93]

Following the 9-11 false flag event,[94] the chief armies for the banking cartel (the U.S., U.K., France, Saudi Arabia, and Israel) targeted every Muslim nation that still controlled its own central bank and currency, and which regulated its own credit (Afghanistan, Iraq, Yemen, Tunisia, Libya). Today, very few sovereign nations remain—Iran, Syria, North Korea, Cuba and Sudan—which the cartel characterizes as the official enemies list.[95]

So, how could these "governments" (the U.S., U.K., France, Saudi Arabia, and Israel) be characterized as religious or spiritual given the usurious practices that rule their monetary systems, from the central banks down to the small-time independent loan-shark operations sprinkled across these territories? Even so-called "Islamic" banks work around the interest prohibition by increasing the principal of loans, which drives the same inflationary results, as well as concentrations of capital into the banks.

---

[92] http://www.nytimes.com/2012/10/24/opinion/who-threw-israel-under-the-bus.html

[93] Israeli Plan to Conscript Ultra-Orthodox Advances
http://www.nytimes.com/2013/05/30/world/middleeast/proposal-for-ultra-orthodox-conscription-gains-traction-in-israel.html

[94] See "Appendix 8—The Anatomy of Treason," in *Solomon's Proof—A Psycho-Spiritual Journey to World Consciousness*, Rabbonai Press, Boulder, CO, 2009. https://www.amazon.com/Solomons-Proof-Rashan-Barcuse/dp/0615185371

[95] http://www.activistpost.com/2012/09/state-owned-central-banks-are-real.html

To see clearly through all these misleading labels, we must re-define the forces at work here.

In theory, major religions agree on interest

Given the historical and contemporary friction between Judaism, Christianity, and Islam—much of it manufactured by those who profit from such—it's important to note the implicit agreement between these "people of the book," the so-called "children of Abraham," on the subject of interest:

> "Thou shalt not lend upon interest to thy brother: interest of money, interest of victuals, interest of any thing that is lent upon interest." —*Deuteronomy* 23:20-21

> "If you have money, do not lend it at interest, but give it to one from whom you will not get it back." —*The Gospel of Thomas* (95).[96]

> "Those who charge usury are in the same position as those controlled by the devil's influence. This is because they claim that usury is the same as commerce. However, God permits commerce, and prohibits usury. Thus, whoever heeds this commandment from his Lord, and refrains from usury, he may keep his past earnings, and his judgment rests with God. As for those who persist in usury, they incur Hell, wherein they abide forever." —*Qur'an*, Al-Baqarah 2:275

The teachings of Christianity are antithetical to usury

---

[96] *The Gospel of Thomas*, as well as other texts found at Nag Hammadi (*Gnostic Gospels*) and Qumran (*Dead Sea Scrolls*), predate the texts that were edited and combined by Bishop Irenaeus of Lyon (3rd Century CE) and the Council of Nicaea (4th Century CE) to form what is currently used as the Christian Bible.

While the Christian churches continue to malign Eastern religions, as we noted earlier it is clear from Jesus' statement—"… whatever you did not do for one of the least among you, you did not do for me …"— that Jesus understood basic Buddhist and Taoist premises, such as the unity of all things[97]; but, he lived in a heathen culture that required physical demonstrations of spiritual metaphors. For example, the graphic story of Jesus casting out the money changers:

> "And Jesus went into the temple of God, and cast out all them that sold and bought in the temple, and overthrew the tables of the moneychangers … And said unto them, 'It is written, My house shall be called the house of prayer; but ye have made it a den of thieves.'"—*Matthew* 21:12

Most notable is the anger expressed in this incident—the use of a whip and in calling the moneylenders "thieves"—underscoring the importance of the moment.

> "If the avatar shows anger, it will be righteous anger, to overcome evil and promote human welfare."[98]

The teachings of Judaism are antithetical to usury

A lot has been made of Judaic law dealing with usury and the pivotal words that prohibit Jews from charging interest to each other, while (in one instance) permitting Jews to charge interest to those outside of the religion. This code was written at a time when Israel and other nomadic peoples consisted of well-defined tribes, and was written to secure the survival of the tribe.

---

[97] One could also say that he understood the African concept of Ubuntu, e.g., "How can any one of us be happy if we are not all happy?"

[98] Howard Murphet, *Sai Baba—Man of Miracles*, The Macmillan Company of India, Ltd., Madras, 1971.

In addition to the prohibition of usury charges to other members of the tribe, another example of such a temporal code of convenience would be the prohibition of homosexuality, because such unions did not result in greater numbers and more soldiers. Both of these codes have shown themselves to be social expediencies, not universal truths. Those who take literally the Torah and its Christian version, the so-called Old Testament, are not able to make the distinction between universal and temporal truth.

Usury was in fact considered immoral by Jews too. If Jesus' examples were not proof enough, the great Jewish theologian, Maimonides, wrote: "Why is [usury] called *nesek* [biting]? Because he who takes it bites his fellow, causes pain to him, and eats his flesh."[99]

> "If thou lend money to any of My people, even to the poor with thee, thou shalt not be to him as a creditor; neither shall ye lay upon him interest." —*Exodus*, 22:25

Survival and revenge

However, usury continued as a means of survival for the Jews (blamed for the death of Jesus by the Romans via Constantine's ideologues[100]), who were ostracized from most professions by local rulers, the church, and the guilds, and then pushed into marginal occupations considered socially inferior, such as tax and rent collecting and moneylending. By serving as money lenders, natural tensions between creditors and debtors were added to social, political, religious, and economic strains between Christians and Jews.[101]

---

[99] Jacob Minkin, *Teachings of Maimonides*, Jason Aronson, 1987, p. 362. Maimonides wrote these words 450 years before Shylock asked for his pound of flesh.

[100] Crucifixion was a Roman punishment for sedition. If Jesus had been punished for blasphemy, as the heavily-edited *New Testament* claims, under Jewish law he would have been stoned to death.

[101] http://www.newworldencyclopedia.org/entry/Anti-Semitism#Restrictions

"... financial oppression of Jews tended to occur in areas where they were most disliked, and if Jews reacted by concentrating on moneylending to non-Jews, the unpopularity — and so, of course, the pressure — would increase. Thus the Jews became an element in a vicious circle. The Christians, on the basis of the Biblical rulings, condemned interest-taking absolutely, and from 1179 those who practiced it were excommunicated. Catholic autocrats frequently imposed the harshest financial burdens on the Jews. The Jews reacted by engaging in the one business where Christian laws actually discriminated in their favor, and became identified with the hated trade of moneylending."[102]

Across Europe, peasants were forced to pay their taxes to Jews, who were economically coerced into becoming the "front men" for the lords. The Jews would then be identified as the people taking their earnings. Meanwhile the peasants would remain loyal to the lords.[103] The resulting antipathy regularly boiled over.

"*SALARINO*: Why, I am sure, if he forfeit, thou wilt not take his flesh: what's that good for?

"*SHYLOCK*: To bait fish withal: if it will feed nothing else, it will feed my revenge. He hath disgraced me, and hindered me half a million; laughed at my losses, mocked at my gains, scorned my nation, thwarted my bargains, cooled my friends, heated mine enemies; and what's his reason? I am a Jew. Hath not a Jew eyes? hath not a Jew hands, organs, dimensions, senses, affections, passions? fed with the same food, hurt with

[102] Paul Johnson, *A History of the Jews* (New York: HarperCollins Publishers, 1987) ISBN 0-06-091533-1, p. 174.
[103] http://en.wikipedia.org/wiki/Usury

the same weapons, subject to the same diseases, healed by the same means, warmed and cooled by the same winter and summer, as a Christian is? If you prick us, do we not bleed? if you tickle us, do we not laugh? if you poison us, do we not die? and if you wrong us, shall we not revenge? If we are like you in the rest, we will resemble you in that. If a Jew wrong a Christian, what is his humility? Revenge. If a Christian wrong a Jew, what should his sufferance be by Christian example? Why, revenge. The villainy you teach me, I will execute, and it shall go hard but I will better the instruction."[104]

In England, the departing Crusaders were joined by crowds of debtors in the massacring of Jews at London and York in 1189–1190. In 1275, Edward I of England passed the Statute of Jewry which made usury illegal and linked it to blasphemy, in order to seize the assets of the violators. Scores of English Jews were arrested, 300 were hanged and their property went to the Crown. In 1290, all Jews were expelled from England, and allowed to take only what they could carry; the rest of their property became the Crown's. The usury was cited as the official reason for the Edict of Expulsion. However, not all Jews were expelled: it was easy to convert to Christianity and thereby avoid expulsion. Many other crowned heads of Europe expelled the Jews, although again conversion to Christianity meant that you were no longer considered a Jew.[105]

In general, though, the inquisitions and pogroms were not successful: usury was used as a weapon by Jews to overcome the limitations of the ghettos to which they were confined, much like African-Americans later used entertainment and sports to escape from the ghettos imposed upon them by whites in the U.S.

---

[104] "William Shake-speare," *The Merchant of Venice*, III, i, 55-75.
[105] For example, the Marranos in Spain.

As Nietzsche notes in *The Genealogy of Morals*,[106] it is this form of revenge that is the basis from which Jesus drew forth his teachings on love and compassion.

The teachings of Islam are antithetical to usury

"O you who believe, you shall not take usury, compounded over and over. Observe God, that you may succeed." —*Qur'an*, Al-'Imran 3:130

Most interestingly, of these three prominent religions, only Islam managed to maintain a semblance of avoiding usury by a work around—increasing the principal on long-term loans, for such items as homes, and by creating banks owned by their respective nations—but, as we already noted in this chapter, almost all of these Islamic banks have been destroyed, or will be, as a direct result of the so-called "war on terror" and "Arab Spring."[107]

If religious teachings do not support usury, who does?

So, if Judaism, Christianity, and Islam do not support usury, then usurers are not, by definition, affiliated with these religions, even if they pose as such. Yet, worldwide, in everyday discourse, religious, and even spiritual, descriptors continue to be applied to persons and nations that practice usury.

---

[106] Friedrich Nietzsche, *The Genealogy of Morals*, translated by Horace B. Samuel, M.A., Boni and Liverlight, New York, 1887.

[107] "The onslaught continues: U.S. Will Grant Recognition to Syrian Rebels, Obama Says": http://www.nytimes.com/2012/12/12/world/middleeast/united-states-involvement-in-syria.html; and *Soros and U.S. Trained Activists in Egypt, Libya, Tunisia, Syria, Iran, Etc To Kill Islamic Banking And State-run Central Banks*: http://www.4thmedia.org/2011/07/soros-and-u-s-trained-activists-in-libya-egypt-bahrain-syria-tunisia-etc-to-kill-islamic-banking/

For example, take the following terms: Rothschild, Israel, United States, Jew, usurer, banker, and Zionism. These are all separate nouns with discrete meanings, yet conflation of these terms with each other is rampant.

From the right, the conflation of these terms produces a voodoo amalgam something like this: Evangelical Christians support Israel, because the existence of the State of Israel is a precondition for the Messiah to incarnate, and the Messiah, to Christians, is Jesus, as he is defined by their churches; and the United States is a Christian nation, so it must support Israel. In this netherworld of logical fallacies, "Render unto Caesar …" is taken literally to mean that what one does in worldly endeavors has no direct relationship with one's spiritual life; thus, for those who fall for this illogical and discontinuous progression of ideas, the rule of law takes a back seat to religious belief systems. Further, since a literal interpretation of the Christian Bible is driven by Creationism, science also takes a back seat to out-of-date temporal metaphors, whenever convenient; otherwise, science is confined to models consistent with the objectives of Evangelical Christianity and the United States; e.g., those of this mental flavor enjoy technological conveniences, but reject the empirical reasoning that created them.

Thus, the conflation of religion, political economy, and science from the right includes: shared pseudo-Judeo-Christian values, an alliance between the United States and Israel, and half-baked science, all of which serve the corporate banking pyramid.

From the left, the conflation produces an alchemical potpourri along these lines: The central bankers, of whom the Rothschilds and the Rockefellers are pre-eminent, control the United States, Britain, France, Saudi Arabia, and Israel, among other nations; in 1948, the Rothschilds funded Jewish terrorists, who ousted the British from Palestine and began the usurpation of private Palestinian lands; Israel should either be wiped out, or there should be a return to pre-1967 borders; all private Palestinian lands should be returned to the previous owners and all Palestinians who lived within borders of Palestine before 1948 should be allowed to return, with full citizenship. In addition, the left sees the right as fundamentalist Christians who support Israel (as a result of being manipulated by Zionists), deny global warming and environmental destruction, oppose birth control and population targets and, as a result, generally support any issues deemed Christian and patriotic by their designated "leaders."[108]

In other words, the conflation of religion, political economy, and science from the left amalgamates anti-imperialist analysis, the United States and Israel and Rockefeller and Rothschild and Christians and Jews, as well as an atheistic science and empiricism into one pot, whether there is any logical connection between the pieces or not.

The upshot of all this conflation, from both the right and the left, is that: the right ignores the problem of usury, because it would conflict with their perception of themselves as religious and moral; while the left ignores history prior to 1948, because it would conflict with their views on imperialism, banking, religion, Jews, and Zionism.

In reality, the governments of the U.S. and Israel—or Britain, France, and Saudi Arabia, for that matter—are controlled by the Anglo-Euro-American banking cartel and its corporations. These countries are not sovereign states, because their currencies are private bank notes. Their foreign and domestic policies are nothing more than a strategy to divide and polarize people, while stealing their assets. Antipathies or agreements between Israel and the U.S., or the other proxies, are manipulated wholly for political purposes.[109] Above all, they worship a commodity defined by usury; that is, the golden calf.

---

[108] http://www.nytimes.com/2012/10/28/opinion/sunday/europes-trouble-with-jews.html

[109] http://www.nytimes.com/2012/11/08/world/middleeast/netanyahu-rushes-to-

Letting the financiers define the issues

Regardless of these important differences—in the way left and right conflate religion, political economy, and science—so-called "liberals" follow the convention of "conservatives" in defining the Middle East in political (nation-state) terms; for example, buying into the so-called "Arab Spring" as a democratic movement. In fact, the uprisings across Arabia (Egypt, Libya, Tunisia, Syria, Iran, etc.) were nothing more than cleverly crafted attacks by proxies for the central bankers to destroy Islamic banking and state-run banks,[110] as well as steal the natural resources and assets of those nations.

> "Middle East regimes threaten to derail the forces of globalization and unseat traditional banking because Islam is setting up an attractive alternate model to conventional banking. Suffering a setback after the "Battle in Seattle", the globalists have wrapped themselves in the cloak of democracy

---

repair-damage-with-obama.html

[110] The MENA (Middle East North Africa) revolutions are from the same playbook as the nonviolent "color revolutions." The playbook is *From Dictatorship To Democracy* by Gene Sharp, of the Albert Einstein Institute (funded partially by George Soros). These revolutions have been successful in Serbia [especially the Bulldozer Revolution (2000)], in Georgia's Rose Revolution (2003), in Ukraine's Orange Revolution (2004), in Lebanon's Cedar Revolution, and in Kyrgyzstan's Tulip Revolution (2005). Iran's Green Revolution (2009) was unsuccessful.

The Guardian reported (November 26, 2004) that the following were "directly involved" in organizing the color revolutions: George Soros' Open Society Institute, the National Endowment for Democracy (NED), the International Republican Institute, and Freedom House. The *Washington Post* and the *New York Times* also reported substantial Western involvement in some of these events. The network for this strategy is outlined in the Carnegie Endowment *For International Peace's Fact-Sheet: U.S. Actors Promoting Democracy In The Middle East*. (Source: http://www.puppet99.com/?p=218, which was taken off the Internet and then reinstituted, in a diluted form, at http://www.activistpost.com/2012/09/state-owned-central-banks-are-real.html.)

to further their agenda. Conventional western bankers see regime change in the Middle East as an imperative to competing with the success of the Islamic banking system."[111]

The corporate media supported these revolutions under the pretense of "establishing democracy and deposing despots," but the real aim initially, of each of these initiatives, is to create chaos and a leadership vacuum, then quickly offer a solution: install a puppet who will do the bidding of the corporate banking pyramid. The citizens of these newly minted colonies are introduced to the illusion of civil liberties, and instead become economic serfs. It's an approach that has been successful across North America and Europe as well.

The correlation between their lack of control over a nation's money creation process by global elites and the resultant implementation of American, and/or European, and/or Saudi Arabian, and/or Israeli aggression—whether economic, political, or military—is clear.[112]

What is the real conflict in the Middle East?

Another example of "liberals" letting "conservatives" define the issues is the so-called Israeli-Palestinian conflict. Sure, Britain and the West drew a bunch of lines in the sand to divvy up the oilfields and to limit the domains of various nomadic peoples, but that does not change the tribal and religious nature of the region.

To say, as the 2012 Green Party platform did, that "… we support equality before international law rather than appeals to religious faith as the fair basis on which claims to the land of Palestine-Israel are resolved," is to pretend that—by ignoring the source of the conflict and

---

[111] Clement Moore Henry, PhD, and Robert Springborg, *Globalization and the politics of development in the Middle East*, Cambridge University Press, 2001, 2nd edition 2010)

[112] http://www.activistpost.com/2012/09/state-owned-central-banks-are-real.html

imposing an artificial political solution—the problem will go away. Not only has this approached failed in the past, it is doomed to fail again, since it frames the issue in old world, European parameters, choosing 1948 as a starting point, because doing so makes it easier to support their position; that is, the Green Party is cherry picking the data, a logical fallacy; for example, they ignore simultaneous expulsion of 850,000 Jews from Islamic nations.[113] What about their rights?

What is being left out of Middle-East discussions?

What all political solutions to the Middle East conflict ignore is that the Levant—at the confluence of three continents: Asia, Africa, and Europe—is a unique sphere and mindset. Opportunistic politicians, failing this understanding and lacking a holistic view of the situation on the ground—as well as in the hearts and minds and collective memory of those who live there—naturally conceive the present antipathy of Islamic, Christian, and Judaic beliefs as irreconcilable; that is, as a religious war between mutually exclusive belief systems. They are correct that it is a religious war, and not a political one, but they are incorrect in believing that this war is irreconcilable and that the only solution is political.

In Singularity we trust

Scientifically speaking, the lack of a religious and/or spiritual solution is impossible, given the omnipresence of the 1st dimension that constantly references the unity within universal diversity. In other words, what physicists call Singularity—which (in time) precedes a "Big Bang" and (in space) exists in the present as the 1st dimension—has essentially the same attributes as what spiritual practitioners call G-d. Any distinctions between Singularity (everything that ever was, is, and will be) and the most generic notion of deity (omnipresence, omnipotence, omniscience) are purely semantic. Thus, following

---

[113] http://www.haaretz.com/jewish-world/.premium-1.629226

Solomon's Proof, any divisions (between science and spirituality, as well as between the various religions) are resolved, if we choose to accept the implications of Singularity; that is, atheism is as outdated as religion.

Judaism, Christianity, Islam, Hinduism, Buddhism, Taoism, and all other religions and spiritual practices worship the same omnipresent, omnipotent, and omniscient state of being (regardless of the constructs they have built around their disparate notions), just as science includes Singularity in the current cosmological model. Thus, in a constantly evolving universe, what was once utopian (the unity of spiritual belief) is now necessary and possible.

For example, let's look at some historical periods in which Jews, Christians, and Moslems—"people of the book"—lived together peacefully in the past.

What enabled them to do so, and what lessons can be derived to carry forward the temporarily successful periods of mutual tolerance from those times?

The golden age of Moorish Spain

Putting aside some exceptions—including a few revolts and periods of religious persecution—Muslims, Christians, and Jews co-existed for over seven centuries in the geographic area known as Al-Andalus or Moorish Spain. The interactions between these diverse social and religious groups resulted in one of the most unique cultures in recorded history, which continued to flourish even after Christians reconquered the territory,[114] until 1492.

---

[114] http://en.wikipedia.org/wiki/Social_and_cultural_exchange_in_Al-Andalus#Social_Interaction

The revitalization of Greece

After the Alhambra Decree (a.k.a. the Edict of Expulsion) promulgated by the Catholic rulers of Spain in 1492, many Jews immigrated to Thessaloniki in Greece, substantially expanding and revitalizing the Jewish community that had resided there for more than 1,500 years. Like many groups in the Ottoman Empire, the Jews of Thessaloniki maintained a traditional culture, which lasted until the middle of the 19th century, when influences from European industrialization and centralization began to take root.

Ninety years after Greece achieved independence from the Ottoman Empire, Jews were made full citizens in the 1920's. With the Nazi occupation of Greece, beginning in 1941, Jews came under increasing persecution and were eventually forced into a ghetto near the railroads in Thessaloniki, from which 60,000 were deported to concentration camps and labor camps, where most died.[115]

The resolution of Christianity and Judaism

As we noted, the division between Christianity and Judaism cannot be plausibly attributed to a difference in way these two religions look at usury (though such an argument is still made by those under the influence of Constantine's version of the Christian Bible, which blames the Jews, not the Romans, for Jesus' crucifixion, and conflates their subsequent persecution with usury).

The historical antipathy between Christianity and Judaism is further complicated by the many Jews who have been duped by Constantine's propaganda regarding the complicity of Jews in the death of Jesus. As a result, Jews have adopted a couple of coping mechanisms: 1) Christianity couldn't be legitimate, because many who claim to be practitioners do not act according to the teachings; and 2) Jesus, despite

---

[115] http://en.wikipedia.org/wiki/History_of_the_Jews_of_Thessaloniki

being the foremost prophet of his time, and despite being from the House of David, could not be the anointed one (messiah), because we have not been liberated—rather, we have been diabolically persecuted. Thus, the derogatory stories that Jews tell of Jesus, particularly the orthodox criticism of his treatment of women as equals, are compensations for the manufactured guilt that has been placed upon them by the editors of the Christian Bible, to facilitate the theft and distortion of his teachings.

The resolution of these two positions requires reconsideration on both sides, as well as from Islam, which springs from the same Abrahamic origins. Indeed, both Christianity and Islam—the world's largest religions as a result of aggressive proselytizing[116] and forced conversions, including torture, inquisitions, and pogroms—have persecuted Jews from their origins to the present, including support from the Roman Catholic Church and the Pope, as well as from the Grand Mufti of Jerusalem, who created, with Hitler's blessing, his own SS brigade (Handzar), for the Holocaust.

Yet, there is nothing in all of the various Christian testaments—including the Christian Bible, the Gnostic Gospels, and the Dead Sea Scrolls—which indicate Jesus is anything other than a practicing Jew. Nor did Jesus, his brother and disciple James, and many others, including a large following of Jews, believe that his message was anything other than one consistent with Jewish law and prophesy.

As noted earlier, Jesus was opposed to the Roman occupation of Judea and was crucified for sedition. That his death did not bring the

---

[116] Turkish children being bought by U.S. armed forces and brought back to the U.S. for conversion to Christianity: https://sputniknews.com/analysis/201801171060827240-turkey-incirlik-children-us-soldiers/. Pope Francis admits Christianity and Islam share similar ideologies regarding proselytizing, while downplaying its effects: https://www.washingtonpost.com/news/worldviews/wp/2016/05/17/islam-and-christianity-both-have-an-idea-of-conquest-says-pope-francis

expulsion of Rome, and the return of the Davidic monarchy as part of a worldwide spiritual pacification, does not invalidate Jesus' relationship to the Jewish prophesies, despite what sectors of the rabbinate may declare. By buying into Constantine's clever edit, they have backed themselves into an intellectual corner without the tools they need to escape.

From our advantageous data promontory two millennia later, we can see both the basis for this schism and its resolution, bringing us to a spiritual synthesis beyond any of these religions, where spirituality and science are different languages for the same reality, a reality that can just as easily be derived and described in political and economic terms, or terms from a myriad of other disciplines.

Science does not support usury, despite corporate spin

Like the cartel from which it receives its financial support, corporate science sells models that are unsustainable. Just as religion and political economy were conflated via the usurers' propaganda, science was absorbed by the corporate banking pyramid, through the stipulations that accompany their funding to universities and research institutes, as well as through ownership of media and publishing empires. Given that the CIA was created from the OSS by doubling the number of agents with former-Nazi spies, is it any wonder that so-called modern science (which has benefited from the classified research of the intelligence organizations) would feel threatened by the convergence of science and spirituality, much as the Nazis were threatened by "Einstein's Jewish Science."[117]

---

[117] http://www.nytimes.com/2012/08/05/books/review/einsteins-jewish-science-by-steven-gimbel.html

A good example of this is the corporate science's current 3-D model of the universe, which imagines it as a phenomenon that expands forever at an increasing rate. Using data and suppositions that amount to tautology, corporate scientists, apparently looking at the asymptotic curves promulgated by their brethren-apologists in the banking and economic communities (who represent interest compounding on global "sovereign" debts in these same impossible terms), seem content that our universe is a one-time proposition unbounded by nature.

But how could this be so if, as Solomon's Proof shows, the extant universe is composed entirely of quanta (what we commonly call light)? Would not then everything behave according to the general protocols of light, even as it becomes more complex? In that likely scenario, the universe behaves as a torus, with creation (white holes) and dissolution (black holes) part of the endless re-cycling of continuous creation.

> "In the face of the totalitarian features of this society, the traditional notion of the "neutrality" of technology can no longer be maintained. Technology as such cannot be isolated from the use to which it is put; the technological "society" is a system of domination which operates already in the concept and construction of techniques." —Herbert Marcuse, *One-Dimensional Man*, 1964

> "Science alone of all the subjects contains within itself the lesson of the danger of belief in the infallibility of the greatest teachers in the preceding generation. Learn from science that you must doubt the experts. As a matter of fact, I can also define science another way: Science is the belief in the ignorance of the experts." —Richard Feynman, 1965 Nobel Laureate in Physics, from "What Is Science?" (1968)

Q.E.D.: Divided We Fall[118]

So, while religion, spirituality, political economy, and science are, ultimately, all reconcilable (by Relativity, Uncertainty, Singularity, and the Quantum-Torus Model), they are not, in any way, to be conflated as labels by which to manipulate the masses.

In other words, in the case of the Levant, the three dominant religions and the various nation-states (including those controlled by the financial powers and those still independent from those powers[119]), must be considered separately, on their own terms, if any solution is to be found to the issues.

And, certainly, any solution must include the elimination of private control over money creation, the powers derived from which are so vast that we must readjust our worldview to comprehend the sinister chokehold over global resources which has resulted, as we see in our next step.

---

[118] *Quod erat demonstrandum* (That which was to be demonstrated).

[119] Israel is a private bank controlled public sector organization where the majority of people are of Jewish ancestry. Syria and Iran are sovereign nations (i.e., they control their own central banks and currencies) where Islam is predominant, and, in Iran's case, in control of the state. Egypt, Saudi Arabia, and Jordan are cartel-controlled, public sector organizations, dominated by Muslims. Palestinians are primarily Muslims who are used by other Muslim nations to maintain pressure on both the entity of Israel and the Jews who live there. Iran and Syria supply a variety of weaponry to the Palestinians, while the United States supplies a variety of weaponry to Israel.

Step 3—Transposing the Money Cartel's Point-of-view

> *What are the roots that clutch, what branches grow*
> *Out of this stony rubbish? Son of man,*
> *You cannot say, or guess, for you know only*
> *A heap of broken images, where the sun beats,*
> *And the dead tree gives no shelter, the cricket no relief,*
> *And the dry stone no sound of water. Only*
> *There is shadow under this red rock,*
> *(Come in under the shadow of this red rock),*
> *And I will show you something different from either*
> *Your shadow at morning striding behind you*
> *Or your shadow at evening rising to meet you;*
> *I will show you fear in a handful of dust.*
> *—T. S. Eliot, The Wasteland, I, 19-30*

The Matrix

Under the poet's red rock, through the rabbit hole, on the other side of the matrix is a reality so different from most folks' perceptions that few are willing to undertake the due diligence to discover what lies there.

Banks and their corporations control the mass media

Instead, their opinions are molded by the corporate-owned mass media, where analysis and reporting take place within an extremely confined ideological framework, as if there are no connections between events— be they political, economic,[120] military,[121] medical, educational,

---

[120] See subtopic "Hiding economic statistics is another weapon in the 1%'s war on the 99%" later in this chapter.

[121] http://readersupportednews.org/opinion2/277-75/30244-exploiting-social-issues-for-militarism-and-imperialism

artistic, athletic, etc.—nor any memory of the past, except where it has been mythologized by those in control.

"History ain't what it is. It's what some writer wanted it to be."
—Will Rogers

"In March, 1915, the J.P. Morgan interests, the steel, shipbuilding, and powder interests, and their subsidiary organizations, got together 12 men high up in the newspaper world and employed them to select the most influential newspapers in the United States and sufficient number of them to control generally the policy of the daily press. ... They found it was only necessary to purchase the control of 25 of the greatest papers. An agreement was reached; the policy of the papers was bought, to be paid for by the month; an editor was furnished for each paper to properly supervise and edit information regarding the questions of preparedness, militarism, financial policies, and other things of national and international nature considered vital to the interests of the purchasers." —U.S. Congressman Oscar Callaway, testimony to Congress, February 9, 1917

"There is no such thing, at this date of the world's history, in America, as an independent press. You know it and I know it. ... The business of the Journalist is to destroy truth; To lie outright; To pervert; To vilify; To fawn at the feet of mammon, and to sell his country and his race for his daily bread. You know it and I know it and what folly is this toasting an independent press? We are the tools and vassals for rich men behind the scenes. We are the jumping jacks, they pull the strings and we dance. Our talents, our possibilities and our lives are all the property of other men. We are intellectual prostitutes." —John Swinton, former Editorial Chief, *The New York Times*, circa 1880, at a banquet in his honor

"A handful of us determine what will be on the evening news broadcasts, or, for that matter, in the *New York Times* or *Washington Post* or *Wall Street Journal*. ... Indeed, it is a handful of us with this awesome power ... a strongly editorial power. ... we must decide which news items out of hundreds available we are going to expose that day. And those [news stories] available to us already have been culled and re-culled by persons far outside our control." —Walter Cronkite, quoted by Carl Jensen in *Censored: The News That Didn't Make the News—And Why*, 1996

"Freedom of the press is guaranteed only to those who own one." —A.J. Liebling

Judging from the editorial limitations of the majority of the so-called alternative media, it is obvious that they are controlled as well.[122] Much of this misdirection is handled by well-placed intelligence agents who double as journalists.[123]

Newspeak

There is a good reason for such censorship policies on behalf of the powers-that-be, for, as Orwell explained, the destruction of language and thought enables the destruction of freedom.

---

[122] http://www.conspiracyarchive.com/2014/01/20/the-gatekeepers-of-the-so-called-left/

[123] http://consciouslifenews.com/inspector-general-fbi-agents-pose-journalists-during-investigations/11126250/#, http://www.digitaljournal.com/news/world/editor-of-major-german-newspaper-says-he-planted-stories-for-cia/article/424470, and http://www.carlbernstein.com/magazine_cia_and_media.php

We realize there are some who will ask, "How does the depiction of events in the mass media destroy language and thought?" Here is our answer.

Nowhere in the mass media will you find a reference to who owns the world's currencies, corporations, and governments; rather, the implication is that the nations of the earth are sovereign, as is their currency and their "sovereign debt." In other words, if you get your information from the corporate media, your worldview is that most nations are self-governing, which means that freedom is a matter of improving governance.

The end of sovereignty

In truth, there are only a few nations left on the planet that can be considered sovereign, i.e., they own their own central bank and they control their own currency—Syria, Iran, North Korea, Cuba, and Sudan[124]—and they are at the top of the bank-owned nations' enemies list.

By creating a false flag event—9/11—and blaming it on Islamic terrorists, those at the top of the power pyramid spread a smokescreen behind which they eliminated state-owned central banks (Afghanistan, Iraq, Yemen, Tunisia, Libya, etc.)[125] that (by not charging interest) were dominating the markets against the usurers' cartel across Asia, Arabia, and North Africa.

What you *will* find in the corporate media, however, are assertions that control of corporations is distributed among millions of stockholders, that elections are verifiable, that the corporate media accurately reports events, that the medical industry is focused on health, that the education

---

[124] https://www.veteranstoday.com/2017/12/01/sudanese-president-to-vladimir-putin-i-need-your-protection-against-the-new-world-order/

[125] http://www.activistpost.com/2012/09/state-owned-central-banks-are-real.html

system is focused on knowledge and empirical reasoning, that the objective of the law is justice, etc.

As things now stand, all of these assertions are patently false. Despite what we were taught in civics and U.S. history classes, the priorities of those who control the playing field are: profit, power, propaganda, and population reduction.

How did this happen?

The power of the international banking cartel begins with private control over money creation. As Meyer Amschel Rothschild, the patriarch of the banking clan that bears his name, is reputed to have said, "Give me control over a nation's money and I care not who makes the laws." Simply put, whoever controls the creation and destruction of a nation's money, as well as credit regulation, controls the government and its citizenry. Today this power rests in the hands of a few families. As we noted in *Step 1*, it was not always this way.

As we've noted, during the early Renaissance, goldsmiths residing in the sovereign monarchies of Europe began lending money based on a fraction of their clients' gold reserves, which the goldsmiths held for "safekeeping." Because these goldsmiths were not licensed bankers, they were loaning what they did not own, i.e., they were counterfeiting: If all the depositors asked for their gold, the goldsmith would be short. Nevertheless, despite occasional runs by their depositors—which, in those days, often resulted in the swift execution of any goldsmith caught short—the profitability of such usury enabled goldsmiths to become royal-licensed bankers, eventually gaining control over the indigenous currencies by luring the sovereign powers into debt, most efficiently by creating wars. Game over.

The bankers soon owned and controlled nation after nation, their power "guaranteed" in perpetuity by control over the central bank and credit regulation. It could be easily argued and defended that *all* of these hijackings of state sovereignty involved unlawful, unconstitutional, and treasonous acts, and that everything which followed is "fruit of the poisonous tree"; that is, without legal standing.

> "Since I entered politics, I have chiefly had men's views confided to me privately. Some of the biggest men in the United States, in the field of commerce and manufacture, are afraid of somebody, are afraid of something. They know that there is a power somewhere so organized, so subtle, so watchful, so interlocked, so complete, so pervasive, that they had better not speak above their breath when they speak in condemnation of it." —Woodrow Wilson, *The New Freedom: A Call For the Emancipation of the Generous Energies of a People*, Section I: "The Old Order Changeth," New York and Garden City, Doubleday, Page & Company, 1913, pp. 13-14.

> "Behind the ostensible government sits enthroned an invisible government owing no allegiance and acknowledging no responsibility to the people." —President Theodore Roosevelt[126]

> "We are grateful to *The Washington Post, The New York Times, Time Magazine* and other great publications whose directors have attended our meetings and respected their promises of discretion for almost forty years. We would have found it quite impossible to develop our global project if we had been subject to the public spotlight during these years. But, the world has grown more sophisticated and willing to move towards a global government that no longer knows war, but only peace and prosperity for all of humanity. The supranational sovereignty of an intellectual elite and world bankers is surely preferable to the

---

[126] Platform of the Progressive Party, "Declaration of Principles," August 7, 1912

national self-determination practiced in past centuries." — David Rockefeller[127]

One of the key events for the banking cartel's implementation and expansion of their criminal conspiracy internationally was the creation of the U.S. Federal Reserve System.

105 Years of Servitude and counting

A little over a century ago, on December 23, 1913, as the Congressional Christmas recess was in progress, a cadre of well-placed operatives for the international financiers, i.e., Representatives and Senators of the United States of America, officially ceded the sovereignty of this nation to a handful of families, who were granted the franchise of creating "legal tender" and regulating credit within these borders.

Despite the legerdemain of their fancy Wall Street lawyers attempting to hide the tentacles of ownership, a study commissioned by the House of Representatives in 1976[128] shows that the original handful of families still control the printing press[129] (the Fed) for so-called "U.S. dollars" (actually, private "Federal" Reserve Notes), which, following

---

[127] June 5, 1991, in an address to the Bilderberger meeting in Baden Baden, Germany (a meeting also attended by then-Governor Bill Clinton), as reported and translated from the September, 1991, issue of the Monte Carlo-based *Hilaire du Berrier Report* (also reported elsewhere in the French press, including *Minutes*, June 19, 1991 and *Lectures Francaises*, July/August, 1991). Mr. Du Berrier closely followed and chronicled the activities of Bilderberg and its overlapping groups, for over four decades.

[128] http://www.scribd.com/doc/46627723/Federal-Reserve-Directors-A-Study-of-Corporate-and-Banking-Influence-Staff-Report-Committee-on-Banking-Currency-and-Housing-House-of-Representative

[129] http://www.scribd.com/doc/12866710/The-ownership-of-the-Federal-Reserve-as-exposed-by-Congressional-Committee-1976

the Bretton Woods conference of June 1944, became the world's reserve currency in the early 1950s.

Leveraging the spoils of this heinous crime, these families and their accessory "subcontractors" have manipulated the money supply and other markets to gain control over most of the key economic assets on this planet[130] and enslave most of the world's population through debt, as confirmed by recent study by Princeton and Northwestern researchers.[131]

Now, over 105 years after the passage of the treasonous and unconstitutional Federal Reserve Act, the ravages of the financiers' strategy are transparent: All resources on this planet—animal, vegetable, and mineral—are valued only according to their profitability. This means *everything*, including water.[132] The cartel tried this trick in Bolivia: the World Bank and the International Development Bank insisted on water privatization as a requirement for Bolivia to retain ongoing state loans. The Bolivian people rejected this psychopathology.[133]

The immortal novelist Charles Dickens understood and captured the gist of the bankers' amoral agenda in his masterpiece, *A Christmas Carol*, in which Ebenezer Scrooge, a usurer in the City of London (i.e., the independent financial district), is confronted by the Ghost of Christmas Future, who lays the responsibility for Ignorance and Want

---

[130] http://www.newscientist.com/article/mg21228354.500-revealed--the-capitalist-network-that-runs-the-world.html

[131]

http://www.telegraph.co.uk/news/worldnews/northamerica/usa/10769041/The-US-is-an-oligarchy-study-concludes.html

[132] http://www.youtube.com/watch?v=7iGj4GpAbTM

[133] http://en.wikipedia.org/wiki/2000_Cochabamba_protests

at the feet of those who profit by the misfortunes that they have deliberately inflicted on others.

Yet, here we are, 175 years after Dickens' account, still looking for a Scrooge conversion on the part of the usurers, who remain content justifying the death and destruction that they have wrought—"to reduce the surplus population," as Scrooge put it—while leveraging their ownership of the mass and social media to promulgate a matrix of clever lies.

What the international banking cartel really represents is the worst in human behavior: fear-based impulses that manifest as greed and self-interest; in other words, devolution via the tyranny of the instincts and ego.

But the source of their power—private ownership of our currency; i.e., our money supply—is only the front end of the problem. As discussed in *Step 1*, the back end is interest charges, levied by the private banks that own the Fed, collected from our once-sovereign and now vassal government in exchange for the "privilege" of using their private, faux "legal tender."

This arrangement is unconstitutional, of course, since Article I, Section 8 requires Congress to issue money and regulate credit, just as Article I, Section 10 forbids the states from issuing their own currency ("bills of credit"); thus, *there is no logical or legal basis for arguing that private parties, such as the Fed, can supplant this sovereign function.* Yet, such is the ubiquity of the cartel's power, including over the judiciary, that their systematic criminal activities continue with impunity.

Lincoln understood this implicitly:

> "That Congress has power to regulate the currency of the country can hardly admit of a doubt, and that a judicious

measure to prevent the deterioration of this currency by a reasonable taxation of bank circulation or otherwise is needed, seems equally clear."[134]

The running tab on bank fraud

The business model for the "too big to jail" banks that own the Fed is fraud, or as Kara M. Stein, Commissioner at the Securities and Exchange Commission (SEC), wrote in her May 21, 2015 dissenting opinion (objecting to the lack of criminal charges against the top executives at the world's largest banks), the behavior of these executives constitutes:

> "... a criminal conspiracy to manipulate exchange rates in the foreign currency exchange spot market ("FX Spot Market"), a global market for buying and selling currencies. Traders at these firms "entered into and engaged in a combination and conspiracy to fix, stabilize, maintain, increase or decrease the price of, and rig bids and offers for, the euro-dollar foreign currency exchange ("FX"). To carry out their scheme, the conspirators communicated and coordinated trading almost daily in an exclusive online chat room that the traders referred to as 'The Cartel' or 'The Mafia.' Additionally, salespeople and traders lied to customers in order to collect undisclosed markups in certain transactions. This criminal behavior went on for years, unchecked and undeterred."[135]

---

[134] January 17th, 1863, in a special message to Congress, quoted in Gerald G. McGeer, *The Conquest of Poverty*, Chapter V, "Lincoln, the Practical Economist," The Garden City Press, Gardenvale, Quebec, 1935.

[135] http://www.ibtimes.co.uk/articles/513606/20131014/fx-market-manipulation-doj-cftc-fca-investigation.htm, http://dealbook.nytimes.com/2013/11/14/u-s-investigates-currency-trades-by-major-banks/,
http://www.nytimes.com/2015/05/21/business/dealbook/5-big-banks-to-pay-

The international banking cartel has been found guilty of—and/or has paid fines, generally without admitting guilt to—crimes affecting virtually every financial and commodities market. The pattern goes something like this: steal hundreds of billions or a few trillion dollars; consolidate the crimes into one case; limit the regulators and prosecutors to a small group; leverage financial power and, if necessary, the threat of "muscle" behind the scenes to arrange for a fine that amounts to mills on the dollar relative to what was stolen; and repeat.[136]

Including and in addition to Stein's citations, the cartel's crimes include, but are not limited to:

- Rigging LIBOR (worldwide interest rates for all debt instruments, including loans, mortgages, and credit cards.[137]

billions-and-plead-guilty-in-currency-and-interest-rate-cases.html, http://dealbook.nytimes.com/2015/02/09/u-s-is-seeking-felony-pleas-by-big-banks-in-foreign-currency-inquiry/, and http://www.dealbook.nytimes.com/2014/11/12/british-and-u-s-regulators-fine-big-banks-3-16-billion-in-foreign-exchange-scandal/

[136] http://www.guardian.co.uk/business/2012/jul/13/libor-scandal-banking-inquiry-whitewash, http://www.nytimes.com/2013/04/23/business/global/stern-words-and-pea-size-punishment-for-google.html, and http://huffingtonpost.com/2010/07/15/goldman-sachssec-settlem_n_648045.html

[137] http://dealbook.nytimes.com/2012/06/27/barclays-said-to-settle-regulatory-claims-over-benchmark-manipulation/ and http://www.guardian.co.uk/business/2012/jul/13/libor-scandal-banking-inquiry-whitewash, http://www.reuters.com/article/2014/04/28/us-sec-rbs-stein-idUSBREA3R1AU20140428, http://coloradopublicbanking.blogspot.com/2015/02/www.nytimes.com/2015/04/24/business/dealbook/deutsche-bank-settlement-rates.html, and http://neweconomicperspectives.org/2015/07/libor-historys-largest-financial-crime-that-the-wsj-and-nyt-would-like-you-to-forget.html#more-9571

- Illegally purchasing U.S. Treasury bonds to keep the government solvent.[138]
- Manipulating the price of gold and other commodities.[139]
- Rigging the municipal bond market.[140]
- Falsifying mortgage securities data to destroy the housing market and reduce home ownership[141]

---

[138] http://georgewashington2.blogspot.com/2009/09/is-treasury-faking-foreign-purchases-of.html, http://www.paulcraigroberts.org/2014/05/12/fed-great-deceiver-paul-craig-roberts/, http://www.dailypaul.com/320958/fed-update-buys-60-of-us-govt-deficit-in-2014, and http://truth-out.org/news/item/9876-the-jpmorgan-derivatives-propping-up-us-debt-why-the-senate-wont-touch-jamie-dimon

[139] http://www.activistpost.com/2014/01/the-hows-and-whys-of-gold-price.html, http://www.globalresearch.ca/financial-criminality-wall-street-manipulates-energy-prices-gold-and-every-other-market/5380325, http://www.nytimes.com/2013/07/21/business/a-shuffle-of-aluminum-but-to-banks-pure-gold.html, www.nytimes.com/2013/09/15/business/wall-st-exploits-ethanol-credits-and-prices-spike.html, http://dealbook.nytimes.com/2014/11/19/senate-report-criticizes-goldman-and-jpmorgan-over-their-roles-in-commodities-market/, http://www.bloomberg.com/news/2013-05-15/eu-oil-manipulation-probe-shines-light-on-platts-pricing-window.html, and http://dealbook.nytimes.com/2013/07/30/jpmorgan-to-pay-410-million-in-power-market-manipulation-case/

[140] http://www.rollingstone.com/politics/news/the-scam-wall-street-learned-from-the-mafia-20120620#ixzz1yS3rPeCP, http://www.maxkeiser.com/2015/02/swimming-with-the-sharks-goldman-sachs-school-districts-and-capital-appreciation-bonds/, http://www.baltimoresun.com/news/opinion/editorial/bs-ed-libor-20120716,0,968211.story

[141] http://www.huffingtonpost.com/2012/01/12/attorney-general-foreclosure-settlement-eric-schneiderman-beau-biden_n_1202643.html, http://www.housingwire.com/articles/33130-doj-fines-jpmorgan-chase-50-million-for-robo-signing, http://www.truth-out.org/buzzflash/commentary/bank-of-america-s-16-8-billion-mortgage-fraud-agreement-is-another-public-relations-

- Selling derivatives to public sector organizations and then manipulating markets to create further indebtedness.[142]
- Manipulating U.S. stock markets.[143]
- Money laundering[144]
- Shielding clients from U.S. taxes[145]
- Corrupting public officials who are responsible for prosecuting corporate crimes[146]

stunt, http://dealbook.nytimes.com/2015/02/03/s-p-announces-1-37-billion-settlement-with-prosecutors/

[142] http://www.forbes.com/sites/halahtouryalai/2012/07/11/city-of-oakland-taps-occupy-wall-street-to-take-on-goldman-sachs/, http://www.law.com/jsp/pa/PubArticlePA.jsp?hubtype=ThisWeek&id=1202612875031&slreturn=20130629162925, http://www.rollingstone.com/politics/news/everything-is-rigged-the-biggest-financial-scandal-yet-20130425, and www.nytimes.com/2014/03/10/business/staking-1-billion-that-herbalife-will-fail-then-ackman-lobbying-to-bring-it-down.html

[143] http://www.rollingstone.com/politics/news/gangster-bankers-too-big-to-jail-20130214 and http://www.opednews.com/articles/THE-U-S-STOCK-MARKET-IS-R-by-lila-york-101227-303.html and http://www.webofdebt.com/articles/computerized_front_running.php

[144] http://www.nytimes.com/2015/03/13/business/dealbook/commerzbank-pays-1-45-billion-to-settle-us-investigations.html

[145] http://truth-out.org/buzzflash/commentary/swiss-banking-giant-helped-us-1-evade-taxes-on-billions-of-dollars-but-justice-department-hasn-t-prosecuted, http://www.theguardian.com/business/2015/feb/08/hsbc-files-expose-swiss-bank-clients-dodge-taxes-hide-millions, http://www.sanders.senate.gov/top-10-corporate-tax-avoiders, and http://www.dealbook.nytimes.com/2014/05/19/credit-suisse-set-to-plead-guilty-in-tax-evasion-case/

[146] http://www.reuters.com/article/2012/01/20/us-usa-holder-mortgage-idUSTRE80J0PH20120120, http://readersupportednews.org/opinion2/277-75/31208-eric-holder-wall-street-double-agent-comes-in-from-the-cold, http://www.truth-out.org/buzzflash/commentary/retiring-obama-administration-prosecutor-says-the-sec-is-corrupt, and

For those keeping score: The cumulative effect of these frauds means that the world's key price benchmarks for interest rates, energy, and currency exchange—as well as all markets (stocks, bonds, mortgages, and other securities and commodities)—are fully compromised, and that those who have profited from these crimes have gotten away with paying only a pittance for their ill-gotten gains (that is, their fines have simply become expenses in their fraudulent business model). Not one of the criminals who directed these conspiracies has served any prison time. In fact, their success has emboldened them.

Hiding economic statistics is another weapon in the 1%'s war on the 99%

But control over all markets goes beyond rigging and stealing; it also serves as a platform for the fabrication of information, as a means of the keeping the populace in the dark as to the cartel's intentions and the true state of the economy, as well as the condition of society in general.

For example, when the Fed stopped publishing its broadest money supply measure, M3, in March 2006, it gave the following excuse:

> "M3 does not appear to convey any additional information about economic activity that is not already embodied in M2 and has not played a role in the monetary policy process for many years. Consequently, the Board judged that the costs of collecting the underlying data and publishing M3 outweigh the benefits."

Some observers claimed that the Fed did this to cover the fact that they were inflating the dollar, but that's old news, since usury must, over

---

time, inflate any currency. There was something else going on.

Behind all this posturing is the simple truth that the measure of the money supply is intentionally obfuscated because the Fed is just one weapon in a much larger coordinated strategy—directed by the self-described New World Order (NWO)[147] (the banking cartel)—to eliminate the last remaining vestiges of public monetary systems and sovereign power, as well as to radically shrink the world's population[148] and make a profit in the process.

Given the cartel's intentional distortion of data, any discussion of statistics, such as that which follows here, should be viewed with these limitations in mind.

Here's a good example of how *The New York Times* operates as a mouthpiece for the NWO, misleading its readers as to what is going on, in this case regarding the condition of the U.S. and world economy. On October 23, 2013, the *Times* ran "Shutdown Will Hinder True Gauge of Economy."[149] Contrary to what the *Times* says, the shutdown over the so-called "debt ceiling"—as well as "sequestration," "austerity," "budget deficits," etc.—is, in addition to serving as an effective distraction from the root cause of global dysfunction (private control over money creation), just an excuse to further decimate the economy, destroy the tax base, cripple the public sector, steal public assets, and, of course, steal private assets as well.

Both the Republicans and the Democrats are owned and operated by the banks and are responsible for jointly executing this strategy. The

---

[147] Both George H.W. Bush and David Rockefeller have used this term to describe individuals and organizations at the top of the power pyramid.

[148] http://coloradopublicbanking.blogspot.com/2013/10/weather-modification-climate-change.html

[149] http://www.nytimes.com/2013/10/23/business/economy/shutdown-will-hinder-true-gauge-of-economy.html

fact that each of these so-called parties has "loss leaders"—for the Democrats it's equality, as in making us all equal slaves, and for the Republicans, it's inequality, as well as the false façade of anti-government slogans, low taxes, and inverted "family values" (which include misogyny, racism, and bigotry), by which they attract different segments of the public to vote for them (and not for an independent third party)—does not make their ultimate objectives different from one another; to wit:

> "When, through the law's intervention, the common people shall have lost their homes, they will be more easy to control and more easy to govern, and they shall not be able to resist **the strong hand of the Government acting in accordance with the orders of the central power of imperial wealth**, under the control of the leaders of finance. ...

> "We'll therefore speed up the question of [fill in the issue] by the political organization called the Democratic Party; and we'll put the spotlight on the question of [fill in the issue] by the Republican Party. ...

> "By dividing the electorate this way, we'll be able to have them spend their energies at struggling amongst themselves on questions that, for us, have no importance whatsoever, and on which we only touch upon as instructors of the common flock."
> —*US Bankers* magazine, 1892 (Sarah E. Van De Vort Emery, *Imperialism in America: Its Rise and Progress*, Emery & Emery, 1893, pp. 71-72, as quoted in the *Chicago Daily Press*)

The bottom line is that the NWO did not want us to know the degree to which they were going to shrink the EFFECTIVE money supply, when they crashed the economy for the 19th time (in 2008), counting from when they successfully hijacked U.S. sovereignty in 1913 with the Federal Reserve Act.

Three charts from 2013,[150] which we are going to describe here, provide the whole story.

First, we have the weekly change rate of the money supply, from 2006 to the beginning of 2013. This can be a little tricky. What is represented is not the actual money supply, but the rate at which it is increasing or decreasing. Beginning in 2008, there was a precipitous decline, which translates as an approximate loss of $3 to $4 trillion in the money supply. Then the supply begins to increase at a much slower rate than it decreased during the crash. This means that the money supply, now $3 to $4 trillion less than when it peaked, begins to grow slowly, never reaching the pre-crash rate. So, despite the growth, the money supply in 2013 was still significantly smaller than it was in 2008.

Next, is a chart from the same period that represents the velocity of money, which is a measure of how quickly the money supply circulates in the economy. After a steep drop following the crash, the velocity continued to slow. Building on the conclusion that we just reached regarding the money supply, this means that whatever small increase in the reduced money supply is happening, it is negated by the loss of velocity. Generally speaking, we can assume that this is because those in receipt of the small increase in the money supply are hanging on to it, or spending it in a way that does not substantively effect the circulation of money. For example, the various iterations of so-called quantitative easing (QE), which were nothing more than the Fed buying toxic assets from the "too big to fail" (TBTF) banks (and sticking the

---

[150] The charts, originally appeared at http://www.nowandfutures.com, which has ceased operations; however, they can be seen on our website, at: http://4.bp.blogspot.com/-SyIqNGLGtpg/UnsOtT4Q_AI/AAAAAAAAASM/Jm-KhwJ1-K0/s1600/money-supply-rate.jpg, http://3.bp.blogspot.com/-TGZWrXblvUo/UnsRmV6_65I/AAAAAAAAASY/m_oy5m_zqbY/s1600/money-suppy-velocity_2006-1.jpg, http://2.bp.blogspot.com/-nupnbWBUTmQ/UnsSYP4OGMI/AAAAAAAAASg/BjMtjKslILc/s1600/unemployment_06-13.jpg.

taxpayers with this sludge). The TBTF banks, in turn, used the cash infusions to buy or seize prime assets at fire-sale prices, as the diminished money supply generated the desired joblessness, bankruptcies, and foreclosures that are the back end of the bankers' "business cycle."

A verification of the effects of a sustained decrease in the money supply can be seen in a third chart, representing the unemployment rate for the same period, which—if those who were laid off and discouraged (after a long period of looking for work) are included—continues to slog along at over 20%![151] Meanwhile, the blue and red masks of the bank party (the so-called "Democrats" and the "Republicans") continue to engage in meaningless staged arguments over distorted statistics.[152] A good example of this partisan volley is the claim that the U.S. economy has recovered[153] while, in fact, about half the nation verges on poverty, and the situation continues to grow worse.[154]

This systematic application of debt slavery applies equally to all domestic and foreign populations in nations where the central banks are privately controlled.

What is the basis of the power of the central bankers?

When private parties own the central bank and literally rent their currency to corporations, governments, and individuals, they eventually accumulate all of the key assets. Revisiting the 2010 study in which three complex systems analysts from the Swiss Federal

---

[151] http://www.opednews.com/articles/Real-Unemployment-at-23--by-Michael-Collins-120909-358.html

[152] http://www.cnbc.com/id/101212564

[153] http://www.nytimes.com/2014/12/16/business/economy/economic-recovery-spreads-to-the-middle-class-.html

[154] http://www.zerohedge.com/news/2015-09-04/record-94-million-americans-not-labor-force-participation-rate-lowest-1977

Institute of Technology in Zurich, Switzerland, inputted the names of those serving on the boards of directors of the most critical 43,060 transnational corporations (TNCs), we see that no more than 147 publicly held holding companies, mostly banks, control the core of the global economy.[155]

Likely, the number of controlling entities is much smaller, but due to the legerdemain of high-priced corporate lawyers via privately and closely held trusts, the exact figure is difficult to glean; although, when interpreted by political economists rather than systems analysts, the analysis clearly supports a structure in which less than 20 shielded holding companies control the 147 public holding companies.[156]

Couple this study with another previously referenced study commissioned by the U.S. House of Representatives Committee on Banking in 1976,[157] and you see that the same handful of families who controlled the Federal Reserve System in 1913 still exert the same power today,[158] through their ownership of the so-called "too big to fail" (TBTF) banks, which are the chief stockholders of the Federal Reserve, based on capitalization. This consolidation is corroborated by a 2010 study of the 50 largest U.S. corporations,[159] which shows that 80% of the cash in the accounts of these 50 mega-organizations was held by the four TBTF banks, Goldman Sachs, JPMorgan Chase,

---

[155] http://www.newscientist.com/article/mg21228354.500-revealed--the-capitalist-network-that-runs-the-world.html

[156] http://www.investopedia.com/updates/rothschild-family-net-worth-explained/

[157] http://www.scribd.com/doc/46627723/Federal-Reserve-Directors-A-Study-of-Corporate-and-Banking-Influence-Staff-Report-Committee-on-Banking-Currency-and-Housing-House-of-Representative

[158] http://www.scribd.com/doc/12866710/The-ownership-of-the-Federal-Reserve-as-exposed-by-Congressional-Committee-1976

[159] http://www.opednews.com/articles/Call-me-crazy-but-I-like-by-Henry-Porter-101202-267.html

Citigroup, and Bank of America.

Why does this mean that the banks control the government?

Once the banks controlled enough Congressmen to pass the Federal Reserve Act during Christmas recess in 1913, and then hoodwink President Woodrow Wilson[160] into signing it, U.S. sovereignty was officially ceded to a few foreign bankers and U.S. industrialists who owned the Federal Reserve System; that is, instead of being able to issue currency without cost (except for the printing), the U.S. government was coerced into issuing Treasury bonds, on which it paid principle and interest, in return for Federal Reserve Notes, which had, as a result of an unconstitutional law, become "legal tender"; in other words, the U.S. government had no choice but to borrow money from the Fed to fund its operations.[161] At this point, U.S. government debt

---

[160] "A great industrial nation is controlled by its system of credit. Our system of credit is concentrated. The growth of the nation, therefore, and all our activities are in the hands of a few men. We have come to be one of the worst ruled, one of the most completely controlled and dominated Governments in the civilized world: no longer a Government by free opinion, no longer a Government by conviction and the vote of the majority, but a Government by the opinion and duress of a small group of dominant men." —Woodrow Wilson, *The New Freedom - A call for the emancipation of the generous energies of a people*, "Chapter VIII, Monopoly or Opportunity?," New York and Garden City, Doubleday, Page and Company, 1913.

[161] One could argue that this process of permanently hijacking U.S. sovereignty began with the 1st and 2nd Banks of the United States (with Alexander Hamilton fronting for the Anglo-Euro-American bankers), followed by the National Banking Acts of 1863 and 1864. In this context, the Federal Reserve Act of 1913 was the final nail in the coffin of U.S. sovereign currency. What we are witnessing today, in terms of the replacement of government functions with corporate control, is simply a charade in which banks and their agents make it appear as if such a takeover is constitutional; however, there is nothing in the Constitution that permits ceding sovereignty (or currency) to private parties. A number of Presidents saw this coming:

began to mount at an asymptotic rate and the U.S. became dependent on the demand for Treasury bonds, a market which is controlled by a couple of the TBTF banks that own the Fed. As noted in the earlier quote from David Rockefeller, this process enabled the central bankers to take control over the government,[162] the operatives of which they handpick, based on the candidate's alignment with their objectives.

> "... Presidents are not elected, but selected by a small elite." — Franklin Roosevelt, in a letter to Edward Mandel House

This control is extended over all three branches of the federal government—legislative, executive,[163] and judicial[164]—including all associated operations, e.g., military and intelligence services, health, education, labor, treasury, etc., as well as the comparable branches of

---

- "I hope we shall crush in its birth the aristocracy of our moneyed corporations, which dare already to challenge our government to a trial of strength and bid defiance to the laws of our country." —Thomas Jefferson
- "Corporations have been enthroned. An era of corruption in high places will follow ... until wealth is aggregated in a few hands ... and the Republic is destroyed." —Abraham Lincoln
- "This is a government of the people, by the people and for the people no longer. It is a government of corporations, by corporations, and for corporations." —Rutherford B. Hayes
- "The real truth of the matter is, as you and I know, that a financial element in the large centers has owned the government ever since the days of Andrew Jackson." —Franklin Delano Roosevelt

162
http://www.telegraph.co.uk/news/worldnews/northamerica/usa/10769041/The-US-is-an-oligarchy-study-concludes.html

163 http://wallstreetonparade.com/2016/10/wikileaks-bombshell-emails-show-citigroup-had-major-role-in-shaping-and-staffing-obamas-first-term/

164 http://www.opednews.com/articles/The-Courts-Like-the-Legis-by-Chris-Hedges-Corporatocracy_FISA_Supreme-Court_Supreme-Court-SCOTUS-150619-168.html

state governments,[165] and key counties and cities.[166] To support this onslaught, police at every level have been internationalized.[167]

There are a few cracks in the facade, which we will discuss later, but for the moment, let's look at how such a power structure operates, as well as the mentality that it engenders and reinforces.

It is important to understand that underlying the use of all information and technology gathered under such a power structure is the *modus operandi* that all data is first vetted for military and intelligence applications, the foremost being weaponry and spying, as well as control of the weather, earthquakes, media, voting, health, education, etc. Before the masses are ever informed about any of these applications, and before any technology is deployed in the public marketplace, it has been thoroughly tested and applied for many years (usually multiple decades) in the service of secret programs. This is the nature of military and intelligence operations upon which power resides in a centralized system such as ours; or, as the military dictum goes, "Intelligence drives operations."

What are the objectives of the New World Order?

---

[165] The state of Colorado serves as an example of how the banks suppress citizen initiatives and siphon taxpayer moneys into corporate coffers. http://coloradopublicbanking.blogspot.com/2014/05/colorado-title-board-reverses-itself.html

[166] For example, the cartel's control over the State of Colorado (documented in the link immediately above) is equally demonstrated by Boulder County and the City of Boulder, which: cooperated fully with the internationally directed purge of the Occupy Wall Street movement throughout Europe and the United States; essentially outlawed homelessness and camping; allow banks and corporations to control their general funds, as well as various social services and police functions (including electronic voting machines). The city's police chief describes his department as a paramilitary organization: https://www.youtube.com/watch?v=7MDseNm86dY

[167] https://www.wsws.org/en/articles/2011/11/occu-n18.html

84

"Some even believe we are part of a secret cabal working against the best interests of the United States, characterizing my family and me as 'internationalists' and of conspiring with others around the world to build a more integrated global political and economic structure—one world, if you will. If that is the charge, I stand guilty, and I am proud of it." —David Rockefeller, *Memoirs*, 2003.

"The nation state as a fundamental unit of man's organized life has ceased to be the principal creative force: International banks and multinational corporations are acting and planning in terms that are far in advance of the political concepts of the nation-state." — Zbigniew Brzezinski, *Between Two Ages: America's Role in the Technetronic Era*, 1971.

On the eve of the Gulf War against Iraq in late 1990, George H.W. Bush stated: "The world can therefore seize the opportunity [the Persian Gulf crisis] to fulfill the long-held promise of a New World Order (NWO), where diverse nations are drawn together in common cause to achieve the universal aspirations of mankind." George H.W. Bush, world-renowned traitor ("October surprise" hostage deal with Iran [with William Casey]), gangster (Iran-Contra drug- and gun-running), murderer (Letelier,[168] among others), and war criminal (first Gulf War and 9-11), apparently thinks himself capable of voicing the universal aspirations of mankind.

The main objective of the NWO is to expand its control over all that it surveys. That much is obvious. But beyond the basics of privatizing all planetary (and extraterrestrial) resources, processes, goods, and services, and having near total surveillance—via satellites, phones, networks, cameras, and drones—what is the point?

---

[168] John Dinges and Saul Landau, *Assassination on Embassy Row*, Pantheon Books, New York, 1980.

In order to justify profiteering by creating war, disease, and ignorance, as well as controlling virtually all key corporations, currencies, markets, and governments, the NWO must necessarily consider itself a cut above the rest of humanity, often referring to its leadership as the "Illuminati." On the surface, the Illuminati is an organization begun in 1776 with the intent of emphasizing reason and rationality. It was forced to disband by the Bavarian state and the Roman Catholic Church.

Whether or not this group continued *sub rosa* is irrelevant because, despite their pretensions, the NWO is neither reasonable nor rational, neither illuminated nor enlightened; e.g., take the activities of the Rockefellers, one of the handful of families that own the Federal Reserve System, as well as some others of their cabal, the Bushes, Mellons, DuPonts, and Henry Ford. All of these folks supported Nazi Germany and eugenics.[169]

"Reducing the surplus population"

Population control is a passion at the top of the power pyramid. To this end, in 1910, the Rockefellers helped fund the Flexner Report, which led directly to control, via licensing (by an Act of Congress), over the medical and pharmaceutical industries in the United States. What we have seen since then is ever-increasing rigidity regarding how disease is diagnosed and what must be prescribed, in order for medical professionals to keep their licenses and insurance (another subsidiary industry of the Rockefeller trusts).

But control over the medical and pharmaceutical industries does not end with the unholy alliance of diagnostic and prescriptive

---

[169] https://en.wikipedia.org/wiki/Rockefeller_Foundation#Overview The Rockefellers supported Joseph Mengele before the Nazis came to power. https://drive.google.com/file/d/1Rb1OY3csfrHNBv8_3UZXW_KljVbl-Gtp/view

profitability.[170] One must also consider the concomitant creation of diseases and their antidotes in the laboratory.[171] While the masses cannot imagine that such programs exist, there is plenty of evidence to be had, beginning with the lab at Plum Island, New York, including:

"... highly suspicious connections between Plum Island and the sudden appearance of Dutch duck plague (1967), Lyme disease (1975) and West Nile virus (1999) on the East Coast. All of these disease outbreaks were first documented within a few miles of the labs. Further, as if the appearance of these foreign disease organisms are not incriminating enough, the sudden and inexplicable appearance of the Lone Star Tick in New York, New Jersey and Connecticut should be, because this sedentary tick species was formerly confined to the state of Texas. Despite the U.S. Department of Agriculture's repeated denials of their work with these organisms at Plum Island, there are documents that reveal otherwise." —from a review of *Lab 257: The Disturbing Story of the Government's Secret Plum Island Germ Laboratory*[172]

And then there are the Rockefeller labs, which have been directly connected to flu,[173] smallpox,[174] and polio outbreaks,[175] not to mention the Center for Disease Control, which created and oversees the Ebola

---

[170] http://thepeopleschemist.com/how-the-ama-hooks-you-on-drugs-harms-your-health-and-hurts-the-earth/

[171]

http://www.naturalnews.com/046290_Ebola_patent_vaccines_profit_motive.html and https://www.nytimes.com/2017/12/19/health/lethal-viruses-nih.html

[172] http://scienceblogs.com/grrlscientist/2007/08/30/lab-257/

[173] http://educate-yourself.org/cn/ottswinefluweapoized1918spanishflu02jun09.shtml

[174] http://www.rense.com/general87/indu.htm

[175] https://www.youtube.com/watch?v=Twch-T-n8Ns

initiative.[176]

The cartel's executive and managerial level operatives continue to be directly involved in these efforts. Bill Gates is a major funding source for programs that tie together weather as a weapon,[177] GMOs, global warming, chemtrails (what government scientists now call "geo-engineering"),[178] and population reduction,[179] all the while making a profit. As if his investments weren't enough proof, Mr. Gates has confirmed his disdain for "excess populations."[180]

The illusion of a democratic republic

This eugenics agenda rarely surfaces in the mass media because, as noted earlier, another key NWO weapon is control over the media, which enables the propagation of information that distorts actual events and conditions.[181]

Such control turns the entire political system into a clever sham. With no limits on election spending, the NWO is able to inundate the population with distortions and sway many unsophisticated voters. Coupled with control over opinion polls and voting machines, as well as voter suppression, voter registration switching, and gerrymandering, it's relatively easy to create the illusion that the political races are closer

---

[176] http://www.naturalnews.com/046941_Ebola_virus_patents_vaccines.html

[177] http://www.geoengineeringwatch.org/massive-us-senate-document-on-national-and-global-weather-modification/

[178] https://www.youtube.com/watch?v=he4TNym-_Jg

[179] http://vactruth.com/2014/10/05/bill-gates-vaccine-crimes/

[180] http://www.dcclothesline.com/2015/06/01/bill-gates-bets-future-epidemic-will-kill-over-10-million-excess-people-are-you-one-of-them/

[181] For example, http://coloradopublicbanking.blogspot.com/2013/11/hiding-economic-statistics-is-another.html

than they really are, which makes the reported results of hacked voting machines and electoral theft[182] seem plausible.

As a result, control over the federal, state, county, and city governments in the U.S. creates a sham gridlock that makes bipartisan compromises in favor of the NWO agenda—e.g., sequestration, austerity, budget cuts, and sale of public assets—seem as if such remedies are the best achievable solutions; when, in fact, they are scripted long beforehand, as a means for reducing and privatizing public services and shifting public tax moneys into private pockets.[183] Again:

> "We must go forward cautiously and consolidate each acquired position, because already the inferior social stratum of society is giving unceasing signs of agitation. ...

> "When, through the law's intervention, the common people shall have lost their homes, they will be more easy to control and more easy to govern, and they shall not be able to resist **the strong hand of the Government acting in accordance with the orders of the central power of imperial wealth**, under the control of the leaders of finance. ...

> "We'll therefore speed up the question of [*fill in the issue*] by the political organization called the Democratic Party; and we'll put the spotlight on the question of [*fill in the issue*] by the Republican Party. ...

> "By dividing the electorate this way, we'll be able to have them spend their energies at struggling amongst themselves on questions that, for us, have no importance whatsoever, and on

---

[182] http://readersupportednews.org/news-section2/318-66/14223-retired-nsa-analyst-proves-gop-is-stealing-elections-part-i
[183] http://coloradopublicbanking.blogspot.com/2013/08/for-profit-banks-admit-failure-seek-to.html

which we only touch upon as instructors of the common flock."
—*US Bankers* magazine, 1892[184]

Such control by privately owned banks, over corporate, government, and political policy continues on an almost worldwide basis.[185]

Profiteering on disease and poisons

Another recent example of such takeovers disguised as "compromises" is the so-called Affordable Care Act (ACA), written by private insurance companies, to benefit themselves, but sold to citizens as a Democratic Party initiative (Obamacare) that aims to help the masses. Whether or not the ACA is an improvement, for those few who can afford it, over what existed before, it is still a scam run by the AMA, pharmaceutical companies, and the insurance industry, to increase profits[186] at the expense of the public's health. No other industrialized nation—except for the Netherlands, where a previously effective health care program was destroyed—allows the healthcare coverage of its citizens to be sacrificed to profit.

In the U.S., however, the profiteering from and destruction of public health is the across-the-board economic strategy of the Rockefellers and their criminal co-conspirators, who control medical, pharmaceutical, and insurance licenses and prescribe the conditions under which they are granted and maintained; for example, anyone questioning why mercury, aluminum, and other poisons are added to

---

[184] Quoted from Sarah E. Van De Vort Emery, *Imperialism in America: Its Rise and Progress*, Emery & Emery, 1893, pp. 71-72, as quoted in the *Chicago Daily Press*.

[185] For example, all European banks followed orders regarding the formation of the EU and the Euro: https://professorwerner.wordpress.com/2015/07/10/hallo-welt/

[186] http://money.cnn.com/2015/01/21/investing/unitedhealth-earnings-obamacare/, http://www.latimes.com/business/hiltzik/la-fi-mh-insurers-are-making-a-mint-from-obamacare-20160216-column.html, and http://newyork.cbslocal.com/2016/10/26/obamacare-premiums-penalties/

vaccines is simply harangued and run out of town, despite the scientific evidence they present,[187] and despite the industry having paid out more than $3 billion in claims.[188]

Another example of criminal corporate takeover, via "agri-business" and the oil-chemical phalanx of the cartel, is the farming industry, where genetically modified crops (GMOs) are not only permitted, but where suppliers, such as Monsanto, are given legal carte blanche to sue farmers for "stealing" their proprietary poisonous pellets, after their fields have been contaminated by airborne GMOs.[189] As noted earlier, regarding gridlocked legislatures and parliaments, the banks and their corporations are succeeding in introducing GMOs into Europe despite the objections of the vast majority of the population.[190]

The examples go on and on, but the bottom line is that the NWO profits while reducing the population through diseases engendered via vaccines,[191] food,[192] and airborne particulates.[193]

---

[187] http://anonhq.com/courts-quietly-confirm-mmr-vaccine-causes-autism/, http://circleofdocs.com/harvard-trained-immunologist-demolishes-california-legislation-that-terminates-vaccine-exemptions/, and numerous other articles.

[188] https://www.hrsa.gov/vaccinecompensation/data/ "Since 1988, over 17,935 petitions have been filed with the VICP. Over that 27-year time period, 16,187 petitions have been adjudicated, with 5,269 of those determined to be compensable, while 10,918 were dismissed. Total compensation paid over the life of the program is approximately $3.6 billion."

[189] http://rt.com/usa/monsanto-patents-sue-farmers-547/

[190] http://www.activistpost.com/2014/02/19-eu-states-reject-gmo-corn-council.html

[191] http://vactruth.com/2014/02/19/cdc-and-emory-university/ and http://kinseimindbody.com/the-debate-is-over-the-mmr-vaccine-can-cause-autism-and-the-cdc-is-engaged-in-a-criminal-conspiracy-to-cover-up-this-fact/

[192] http://naturalsociety.com/new-study-monsantos-herbicide-chemical-damages-dna/ and http://www.larouchepub.com/other/1995/2249_kissinger_food.html

[193] http://www.mayanmajix.com/art2152.html

Weather modification, climate change, catastrophic events, advanced weapons, and population reduction

Additionally, for many decades, the cartel's military and intelligence organizations have been fine-tuning the manipulation of climatic and geologic events. Before you invoke the *ad hominem* "conspiracy theory" regarding these claims, remember that, in a real debate, you lose points for calling your opponent names, appealing to emotions, or using a host of logical fallacies instead of presenting facts to back your proposition.[194] Once you engage in such an approach, your argument can never claim to be logical.

Most people have a hard time believing that the weather and cataclysmic events could be precipitated by anyone other than Mother Nature: the power unleashed by these phenomena seems off the scale of human invention.

Of course, folks thought the same way about Einstein's claim regarding $E=mc^2$; after all, how could a few pounds of plutonium level a city?

However, various sources confirm[195] that all it takes is about a billion volts, directed at the ionosphere,[196] to alter the jet stream and move weather fronts, including hurricanes.[197] Earthquakes, too, can be induced by other types of electromagnetic waves. This may seem less shocking (no pun intended), since seismologists have been

---

[194] http://www.informationisbeautiful.net/visualizations/rhetological-fallacies/ and https://yourlogicalfallacyis.com/

[195] http://beforeitsnews.com/earthquakes/2015/09/the-new-warfare-of-unnatural-disasters-death-by-earthquakes-tsunamis-and-volcanoes%E2%80%8F-2546580.html and http://beforeitsnews.com/chemtrails/2015/06/conspiracy-theorists-label-still-used-in-spite-of-obvious-and-verifiable-geoengineering-realities-2449796.html

[196] http://globalresearch.ca/articles/CHO409F.html

[197] http://beforeitsnews.com/police-state/2015/06/the-un-is-planning-to-migrate-americans-from-california-followed-by-the-entire-southwest-1622.html

precipitating temblors for some time.[198] Fracking serves as another obvious example of how relatively low-energy triggers can induce temblors. Programs for weather modification and weather-as-a-weapon were openly discussed in the U.S. Senate as far back as 1978[199] and within the scientific community at least as far back as 1958.[200]

By 1999, the European Union parliament was aware of the U.S. deployment of these weapons, and asked the United States to come clean[201] about its HAARP (High Frequency Active Auroral Research Project[202]) program. Three years earlier, the Canadian Broadcasting Corporation (CBC) asked similar hard questions in a documentary on HAARP.[203]

Both groups were stonewalled. Even today, 21 years after the CBC documentary, the banks' vassal "U.S. government" apparatus still insists that these weapons are for peaceful purposes. However, as noted by a retired, high-ranking U.S. military intelligence officer in the CBC documentary, the military never limits technology to peaceful purposes.

For example, in 1969, when students protesting U.S. imperialism in Vietnam took over the Applied Electronics Laboratory at Stanford University, they discovered in the files a research project in which the

---

[198] http://www.bariumblues.com/earth_as_a%20_weapon.htm and http://www.nytimes.com/2013/12/13/science/earth/as-quakes-shake-oklahoma-scientists-eye-oil-and-gas-industry.html and https://www.dailykos.com/story/2015/02/23/1366282/-U-S-Geological-Survey-Fracking-waste-is-the-primary-cause-in-dramatic-rise-of-earthquakes

[199] http://www.geoengineeringwatch.org/massive-us-senate-document-on-national-and-global-weather-modification/

[200] http://activistpost.net/Can-We-Survive-Technology.pdf

[201] http://exonews.org/european-parliament-issues-warnings-on-haarp/

[202] http://www.mondovista.com/haarp00.html

[203] http://www.youtube.com/watch?v=QkLTzesBxGE and http://www.youtube.com/watch?v=Zi1nLmlicxU

application of electromagnetic frequencies originally designed to treat heart disease were also employed to cause heart attacks. As similar facts were accumulated from the laboratory's records, it became clear that all high-level secret research is always first vetted for military and intelligence applications.[204]

To the financiers who run the show, their enemy is any person, group, or body corporate and politic—allies included—who represent a threat to their private hegemony over the world. There's no telling what global population number would satisfy the Rockefellers' and their fellow elitists' vision of a suitable master race, after all, secret societies depend on secrecy, but our best guess, based on various sources and the current strategy of the "New World Order," is that between 450 and 550 million people, or roughly 1/14 of the current world population, is their goal.

Given this shocking figure, it seems logical to ask how the .000001% plan on reducing our numbers. As we've observed, they have lots of options: inciting war; spreading disease; poisoning the air, water, and earth; genetically modifying and poisoning the food chain[205]; triggering cataclysms masquerading as weather aberrations and earthquakes[206]; destroying economies[207]; and engineering drought and starvation.[208]

According to a variety of estimates, the technology at the NWO's

---

[204] A recent example, via an admission by U.S. Defense Secretary Jim Mattis: https://www.activistpost.com/2017/09/us-defense-secretary-jim-mattis-weighs-using-kinetic-weapon-north-korea.html

[205] http://www.globalresearch.ca/monsanto-the-tpp-and-global-food-dominance/5359491

[206] http://www.infowars.com/haarp-hurricane-irene-and-the-dc-earthquake-%E2%80%A6connected/

[207] http://en.wikipedia.org/wiki/Confessions_of_an_Economic_Hit_Man

[208] http://andrewgavinmarshall.com/2013/01/29/the-financialization-of-food-and-the-profitability-of-poverty/

disposal generally runs 35 to 45 years ahead of public knowledge; so, on-going hits using atmospheric and geophysical weaponry are naively taken as natural events by the public.

Summary

Going back once more to David Rockefeller's quote, we see that the NWO believes it has the power to eventually subdue the remaining pockets of sovereignty and have the entire planet at its merciless beck and call; and, while we may see those folks at the top of the power pyramid who are perpetrating this agenda as completely immoral, they themselves operate in a completely *amoral* world of "technical decision making." Yet, it is our hope, as Shelley noted in *Ozymandias*, that their hubris is nothing more than "famous last words."

I met a traveller from an antique land,
Who said—"Two vast and trunkless legs of stone
Stand in the desert. ... Near them, on the sand,
Half sunk a shattered visage lies, whose frown,
And wrinkled lip, and sneer of cold command,
Tell that its sculptor well those passions read
Which yet survive, stamped on these lifeless things,
The hand that mocked them, and the heart that fed;
And on the pedestal, these words appear:
My name is Ozymandias, King of Kings;
Look on my Works, ye Mighty, and despair!
Nothing beside remains. Round the decay
Of that colossal Wreck, boundless and bare
The lone and level sands stretch far away."
—Percy Bysshe Shelley, *Ozymandias*

What are our alternatives?

STEP 4—MAKING MONEY A PUBLIC UTILITY THROUGH SUSTAINABLE ECONOMICS

And Jesus went into the temple of God, and cast out all them that sold and bought in the temple, and overthrew the tables of the moneychangers ... And said unto them, "It is written, My house shall be called the house of prayer; but ye have made it a den of thieves."
– Matthew 21:12-13

For-profit banks admit failure; seek to destroy public banks

As we detailed in the previous chapter, the international banking cartel sees itself as the entitled and rational overlord of planetary operations and the direction of human evolution. The core problem with their point-of-view is that these individuals are handicapped by stunted mental and emotional development.

By describing those at the top of the power pyramid as handicapped because their consciousness rarely uses portions of the brain that connects individuals to one another in a meaningful way,[209] we mean to say that they lack the ability to think and behave holistically. Much like babies who are not held enough and do not bond with other humans, the financiers behave as if they are the only ones that matter.[210]

---

[209] https://www.ted.com/talks/jill_bolte_taylor_s_powerful_stroke_of_insight

[210] "Economic crisis — impaired brain function a major cause?" (https://drgrandville2.wordpress.com/2008/10/21/financial-crisis-impaired-brain-function-a-major-cause/) and "Wealthy Stockbrokers More Dangerous Than Psychopaths" (http://readersupportednews.org/news-section2/320-80/7784-

They believe that they are "the best and brightest" and "the smartest people in the room," but their limited brain and heart functionality reveals they are literally half-wits. They flatter themselves into believing they are the Illuminati, but have no idea what such an enlightened state would entail.

Since these self-described Illuminati are devoid of attachments to human beings outside of their own limited circles (if that), they possess no moral compass to limit their crimes against humanity. The focus of their forceful control is "the masses" (labor); or, as the they see it, the required number of debt slaves to keep their self-serving apparatus operating (and for a few, to serve as the .000001%'s military and police enforcers), as well as to create product and spend their earnings to consume those products (and to go into further debt to do so), as a material reward for their servitude.

> "If ye love wealth greater than liberty, the tranquility of servitude greater than the animating contest for freedom, go home from us in peace. We seek not your counsel nor your arms. Crouch down and lick the hand that feeds you. May your chains set lightly upon you; and may posterity forget that ye were our countrymen." —Samuel Adams

So ubiquitous is the cartel's criminal conspiracy that they are in the process of outlawing all alternatives. For example, take the temporarily suppressed Trans Pacific Partnership (TPP) agreement, negotiated in secret, which Obama insisted he would sign, if it got to his desk. As noted by Sam Knight:

> "Publicly owned enterprises, for example, are being targeted by negotiators. One such entity in the United States that has been the subject of considerable interest in recent years is the Bank of North Dakota (BND) -- the only fully publicly owned

---

study-wealthy-stockbrokers-more-dangerous-than-psychopaths)

financial institution in the country. The BND, which is only allowed to lend wholesale, was a stabilizing force that helped keep the already energy-rich state insulated from the shock of the financial crisis (Alaska, for example, didn't fare as well). It has also brought a small fortune to the state's treasury -- $340 million in net tax gain between 1997 and 2009. Legislators in at least 13 different states have proposed studying or emulating the North Dakota model -- state-owned development of central-bank style institutions guaranteed by tax revenue. But if the TPP is passed, that option might not be available. (Barbara) Weisel (the United States Trade Representative's chief TPP negotiator) said that State Owned Enterprises (SOE) are routinely "competing directly with private enterprises, and often in a way that is considered unfair."

"Some of the advantages that can be conferred on State Owned Enterprises are things like preferential financing," Weisel said. "Those are things that wouldn't be provided to private companies -- preferential provision of goods and services provided by a government."

She said that "State Owned Enterprises -- which in some cases can comprise a significant percentage of an economy -- can be used to undermine what we're otherwise trying to gain from this free trade agreement."

A spokesperson for the BND declined to comment on whether or not this outlook was perceived by the bank to be an institutional threat. But, depending on the report's language, foreign bankers could claim that the BND stops them from lending to commercial banks throughout the state.

Citigroup's Johnston, in response to another question from the audience, said that corporations weren't exactly enamored of competition with publicly owned enterprises -- and that they are prodding TPP delegates into doing something about it.

"The companies that are running up against the problem and the challenges of the state-owned enterprises, they obviously feel strongly enough about it that the problem is being addressed within the negotiations," he said."[211]

In other words, as Rudy Avizius notes in *New World Order Blueprint Leaked*, "If implemented, this agreement will hard code corporate dominance over sovereign governments into international law that will supersede any federal, state, or local laws of any member country." A recent example of this is the attempt to destroy the United States Postal Service, by saddling it with the stipulation that it must fund its pension 75 years in advance, at the same time that banks and their corporations are raiding Social Security and their own workers' pension funds.[212] Thankfully, the opposition in other nations nixed this corporate-led coup d'état masquerading as a treaty.

There it is, the heart of the banks' failure: The inefficiencies of managing the world's resources for the benefit of a small group of psychopaths is laid bare; their criminal operations cannot compete with enterprises managed in the public interest; so, they must attempt, with whatever faux legitimacy they can conjure, to make it illegal for public bodies to remain sovereign—independent of the banks and their corporations—and manage resources in the public interest.

This is one of the textbook definitions of fascism: Corporate control over the state, an agenda that has been laid bare in recently revealed

---

[211] http://truth-out.org/news/item/15142-corporate-backed-trans-pacific-partnership-shrouded-in-secrecy
[212] http://nhlabornews.com/2013/08/senator-carper-introduces-legislation-to-virtually-end-the-usps/

secret documents from another trade treaty.[213]

From colonial times to the present, the usurers have destroyed U.S. sovereignty, bit by bit, with TPP the latest and most insidious illegal attempt. Indeed, as we shall see in *Step 6*, all "legal" justifications for the cartel's control are, metaphorically speaking, "fruit of the poisonous tree,"[214] meaning that the cartel's assets and power are the result of a series of unconstitutional and/or otherwise illegal actions; thus, the entire chain is invalid and without merit.

Yet they continue down this illegitimate path because they know that to maintain power they must use smoke and mirrors to cloud the true nature and effects of their policies and pathology. The fact is, any economy based on private currency and interest charges is certain to crash on a regular basis, after it has destroyed the livelihoods and lives of those whom it enslaves. This has been common knowledge for ages. That is why, as the Torah notes, jubilee years were implemented on a regular basis, to reset systems in which usury and other forms of slavery were practiced.

The eclipse of usury

And what do the usurers put above the rights of people? Mammon. The Golden Calf. Gold. Capital (money that has been commoditized through usury). In the Christian *Bible*, this issue comes to a definitive head in the story of Jesus driving the money changers from the Temple with a whip and calling them "Thieves!" This took place in 33 CE, while the Roman Empire was suffering from a depression as a result of

---

[213] http://www.thedailybell.com/news-analysis/leaked-tisa-docs-part-of-secret-global-constitution/

[214] A legal term used to describe a situation in which tainted evidence or illegal actions by "the authorities" invalidate any evidence that follows.

the widespread practice of usury: As we noted previously, every member of the Roman Senate at that time was a usurer.[215]

Clearly, Jesus (or the author of that story, take your pick) understood that the moment in which interest is charged on money, money turns into capital and becomes an object (commodity) that is valued above people, while labor is simultaneously devalued and commodified.[216]

The mathematics underlying this problem and its solution are relatively simple, but before your eyes glaze over at the mention of economic analysis, consider a choice quote that we repeat from *Step 1*:

> "If economists can't say what they mean in simple, clear terms, then either there is something to be gained from mystifying what they are doing, or they themselves do not really understand what they claim to understand." —Rosa Luxemburg

In deference to this quote, let's look at a few permutations and combinations of private and public currencies and banking, to see (in a few pages of text and three graphs) which combination is capable of producing a sustainable economy and stable currency. Notice how the models follow the concentric pattern of Copernicus' rendering of the heliocentric solar system, which we discussed in the *Prologue*.

---

[215] *Observations on: I. The Answer of M L'Abbé de Vertot to the late Earl Stanhope's Inquiry concerning the Senate of Ancient Rome, dated December 1719; II. A Dissertation upon the Constitution of the Roman Senate, by a Gentleman, published in 1743; III. A Treatise on the Roman Senate, by Dr. Conyers Middleton, published in 1747; IV. An Essay on the Roman Senate, by Dr. Thomas Chapman, published in 1750; by Mr. Hooke, published in 1758*, specifically "Observations of Dr. Middleton's Treatise and Dr. Chapman's Essay on the Roman Senate," p. 189.

[216] That is, the value of labor must be less than the value of labor plus compound interest; or, to put it mathematically, $P < P + I$.

Private banking with interest

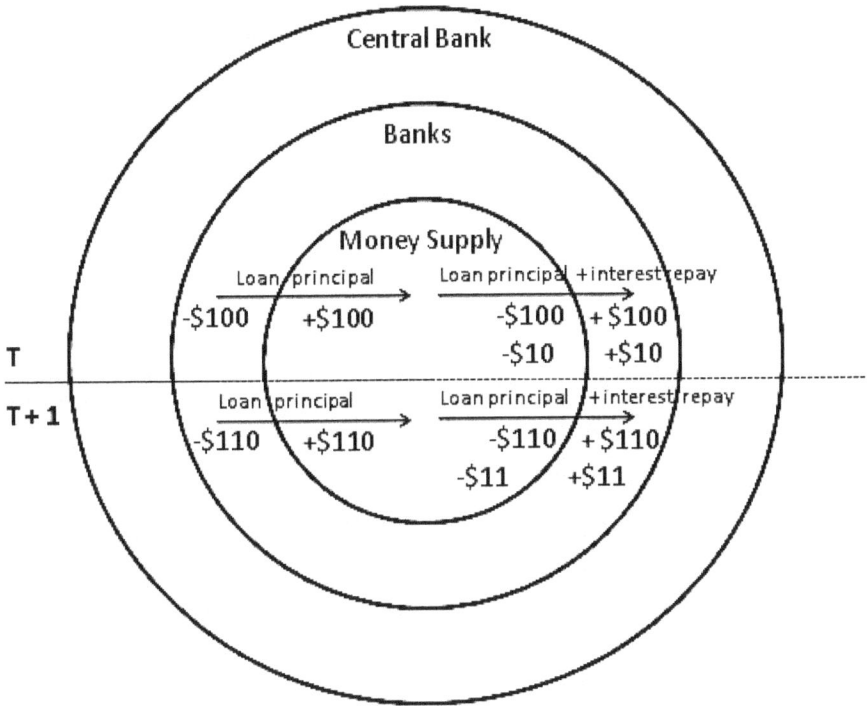

Commentary: T = Time, so the events above the dotted line represent the initial interval or event, and the events below the dotted line represent the subsequent interval or event.

In the first interval (T), a commercial bank creates a loan of $100, which temporarily increases the money supply by $100. When the loan is repaid (at 10% interest), the money supply is reduced by $100, with the original loan (bank money) being extinguished, plus a further reduction of $10 in the money supply (because the money to pay the interest is never created with the loan), which becomes the property of the commercial bank, to distribute or invest as it chooses.

In the second interval (T + 1), the commercial bank continues to inflate, then deflate, the money supply by choosing to leverage its $10 in interest income toward increasing its loan portfolio, so it loans $110 dollars and temporarily increases the money supply by that amount. When the loan is repaid (at 10% interest), the money supply is reduced by $110, with the original loan (bank money) being extinguished, plus a further reduction of $11 dollars from the money supply (since the money to pay the interest was never created), which becomes property of the commercial bank, to distribute or invest as it chooses. As you can see, after each interval, the money supply is reduced by an ever-increasing amount, which represents the growing private bank ownership over the money supply and the assets generated therefrom.

During the part of the "business cycle," when the money created from loans is increasing, the process seems to work fine, because there is an increasing amount of money in circulation to pay the interest. But when the private banks choose to deflate the money supply by calling in their loans, the money supply is reduced by the principal of all the loans (bank money) plus the interest on those loans, which, if and/or when collected, will belong to the commercial banks, to distribute or invest as they choose. Under these conditions, there is no longer enough money to pay for all the principal and interest (since the money to pay the interest was never created), leading to bankruptcies, foreclosures, and joblessness, which enables the commercial banks to buy the collateralized assets ("the fruits of our labor," which they have amalgamated through loans) at fire sale prices.

To recap, with privately owned banks and interest, an increasing amount of debt (loans) is needed to maintain or grow the money supply during the inflationary part of the "business cycle," to pay off the interest. Following this, an event (say, the 2008 collapse of Lehman Brothers) is created as an excuse to constrain credit and reduce the money supply, thereby enabling the banks to repossess the collateralized assets backing the loans; or, if these are insufficient to cover the losses, any other available assets.

Whether the big banks that own the Fed recover their losses in this situation is immaterial, since for them the privately owned central bank is the lender of last resort and is used by these "too big to fail" private banks, as a backstop to prop them up following each crash, and to reset themselves, fully liquid and ready to buy up assets for pennies on the dollar, after destroying massive amounts of real value throughout the rest of the system. This destructive reset, in a capitalist system (i.e., privately owned money creation), is necessary because of all the counterfeit (false) value created by interest. Interest, then, is the poison pill by which the value created by labor is stolen, simultaneously devaluing labor.

Public central banking with interest

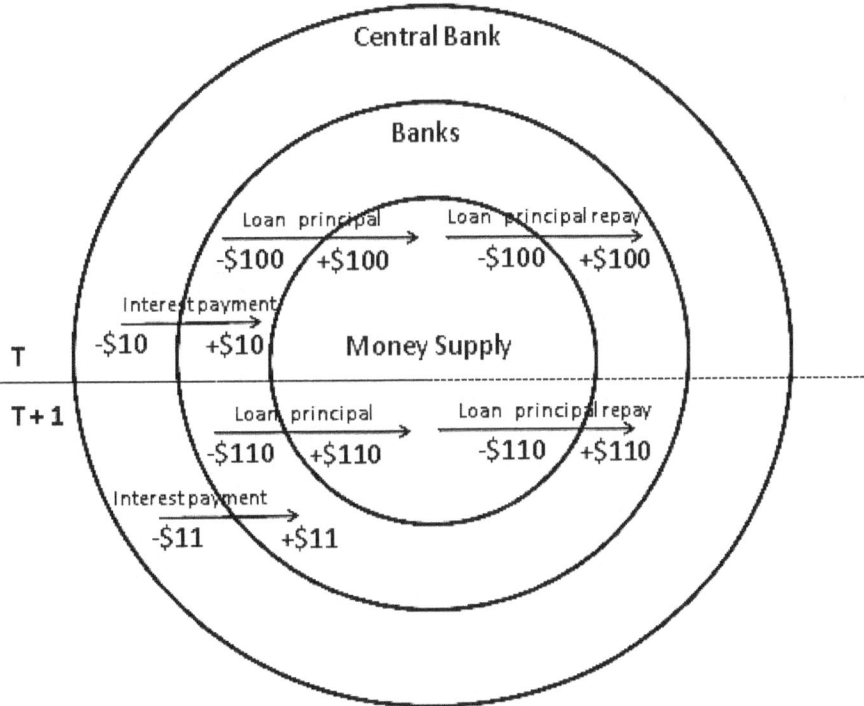

Commentary: T = Time, so the events above the dotted line represent the initial interval or event, and the events below the dotted line represent the subsequent interval or event.

In the first interval (T), a commercial bank creates a loan of $100, which increases the money supply by $100. When the loan is repaid, the money supply is reduced by $100 and the public central bank (paying the 10% interest) makes a $10 deposit with the private commercial bank.

In the second interval (T + 1), the private commercial bank continues to inflate and deflate the money supply by choosing to leverage the $10 it made in interest income by increasing its loan portfolio, so it loans $110 dollars and increases the money supply by that amount. When the loan is repaid, the money supply is reduced by $110 and the public central bank makes an $11-dollar deposit (paying the 10% interest) with the private commercial bank.

In this scenario, when the commercial banks choose to deflate the money supply by calling in their loans (based on whatever excuses they believe the public will buy, with orchestrated coaxing from the mass media that they own), the money supply is reduced by the principal of all the loans, but not the interest on those loans, since the public central bank has added to the money supply by paying the private commercial banks an amount equal to the interest charged. The banks retain this interest income during contractions, to buy assets from the jobless, bankrupt, or foreclosed victims for pennies on the dollar. Therefore, the shrinkage of the money supply would be of a magnitude similar to the private central banking system in the previous example. However, in this case, the public central bank would have the option of providing counter-cyclical programs to replenish the money supply (though this would not cure the problem of inflation, since money [interest payments created by the central bank] was added to the supply without adding value [labor]); that is, more money is chasing the same amount of goods and services.

In addition, further inflationary pressures would be generated because there would continue to be an impetus for the private banks to expand

and contract the money supply for profit and "asset acquisition." Since profit on loans are one of the means by which private banks stay in business, in this scenario, withholding the infusion of money by the public central bank to pay interest on loans would not be an option. In other words, even with the best-case scenario of a public central bank creating money to pay the interest on loans, a system that includes for-profit banks and usury leaves private parties in in control of the money supply, i.e., its creation and regulation, and therefore its manipulation for profit, rather than as a public utility managed in the public interest.

The solution to the inflationary problem illustrated in this model (base money paid by the central bank to cover the interest payments to the commercial banks) seems to call for the central bank to spend the so-called "cost of the loans" (compound interest) directly into the money supply, through public projects (goods) and/or social programs (services), rather than paying these costs directly to the commercial banks (which use them to manipulate the money supply); however, if such were the case, the commercial banks would be relegated to nothing more than pass-through institutions, merely administering loans without any profit, i.e., they would go broke (by private banking standards), or at least be operated on a "cost-plus" basis (the cost of providing goods or services, plus, say, 6% of that cost, as a profit margin (not as compound interest). This conversion of private banks dependent on profits generated by compound interest into banks that serve an administrative or pass-through function, begs our next model, where commercial banks are replaced by state-, county-, and municipal-owned banks that are members of a regional branch of the publicly owned central bank.

Before we detail that model, it's worth noting that if the public-private ownership model illustrated in the above example were reversed, with a privately owned central bank and the rest of the system consisting of public banks—owned by states, counties, cities, and other political subdivisions (tax districts)—the inflationary outcome is accelerated, with the public banks forced to charge interest to pay off their loans from the central bank, thus generating an ever-accelerated destabilizing force that eats away at the money supply, transferring large portions back to the private parties that own the central bank. Additional inflationary forces would result from the government having to issue bonds and pay interest (since the government would not have its own sovereign currency) in order to generate privately issued central bank notes ("Federal" Reserve Notes, etc.) to pay its debts, or buy goods and services.

In either case, public-private or private-public "partnership," yet another potential source of inflation is the loans by commercial banks that go unpaid during economic contractions, thus increasing the money supply without being extinguished upon repayment. Admittedly, it could be argued that this surplus currency is far offset by the shrinkage of the money supply as credit evaporates, and as assets (funded by the loans) are seized by the banks; however, the inflationary effects of interest on the cost of goods and services created by any individual or corporation with a debt service (i.e., interest expense) would remain.

As always, with private central banks, war profiteering, in its many forms, including economic predation in all major industries, would continue, and government debt would soar correspondingly, borrowing to pay for services mandated by corporate control over banking and governments. Again, corporate control over the state is one of the definitions of fascism.[217]

---

[217] George H. Sabine, *A History of Political Theory*, Holt, Rinehart and Winston, New York, Third Edition, 1961, p. 919. Thus, Lenin's notion that imperialism is the final stage of capitalism falls short; rather, the final stage of capitalism is fascism, a form of totalitarianism.

Public banking without interest

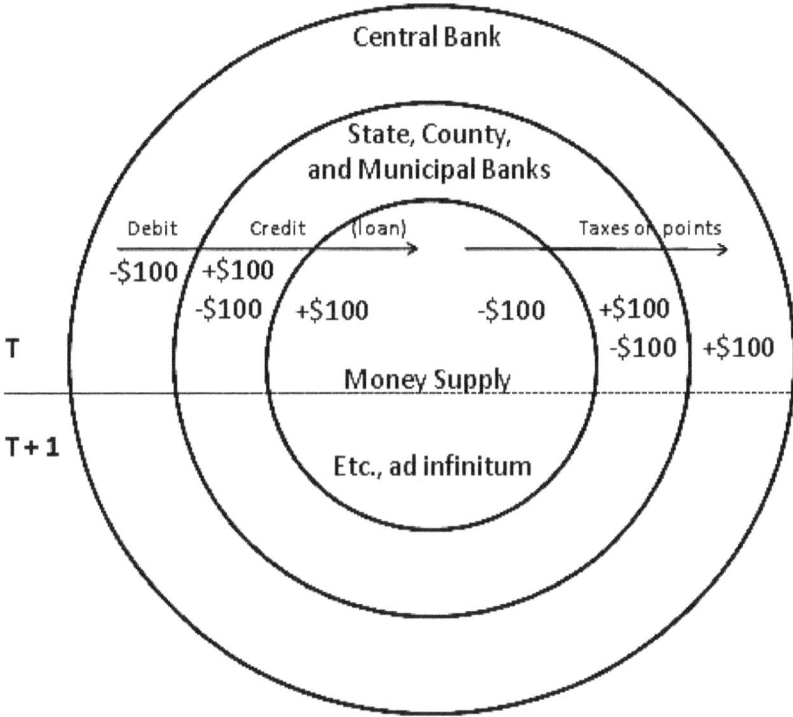

Commentary: T = Time, so the events above the dotted line represent the initial interval or event, and the events below the dotted line represent subsequent intervals or events.

In this model, private for-profit banks have been phased out of existence. The nation's banks now consist of a publicly owned central bank (which is simply the nation "doing business as" [d/b/a] a bank) and publicly owned state, county, and municipal banks, and subsidiaries, as well as public banks formed by other political subdivisions that meet minimum capitalization requirements. In this case, with private banks no longer in the business of governance and no longer using compound interest as a means of inflating and deflating the value of the currency relative to goods and services, or to steal the value created by labor, the options for monetary policy improve significantly.

First, interest can be eliminated, as was recently proposed in Russia.[218] As noted in *Step 1*, interest is, in the end, nothing more than a mathematical trick, which does not represent the cost of creating money. Eliminating interest would return sovereignty to the people, instead of allowing a few bank holding companies to dictate global policy. As it currently stands, there are nations that have publicly owned central banks and yet are not sovereign nations, in that they still issue bonds and pay interest to private parties that hold the bonds, which act as collateral for the receipt of private bank notes. But as we've noted, privately owned for-profit banks are not businesses. They are unconstitutional as well as fraudulent criminal enterprises that, by design, aim to destroy sovereignty and steal assets. It's also worth noting that the elimination of interest would not change the motivation of borrowers, since a good credit score would remain one of the basic qualifiers for borrowing within a publicly owned banking system.

Second, each political subdivision, working in concert with its own bank (or a bank owned by another political subdivision), may create credit through zero-interest loans; however, these political subdivisions (states, counties, municipalities, and other taxing districts) would be subject to balanced budgets and non-inflationary credit policies, evaluated by an analysis of the local price index (LPI), based on a basket of goods deemed to be necessary for "life, liberty, and pursuit of happiness" of the inhabitants. In other words, an economic bill of rights would determine the basket of goods and services to which the sovereign currency would be indexed (for example, food, clothing, shelter, healthcare, education, access to cultural tools, etc.), thus guiding the central bank as to the inflationary or deflationary pressures on the currency in local markets. Adjustments to the money supply

---

[218] http://journal-neo.org/2015/11/22/russia-debates-unorthodox-orthodox-financial-alternative/

could be made by (1) increasing or decreasing the availability of local credit, (2) by increasing or decreasing taxes at any level (city, county, state, or nation), (3) by the federal government spending base money directly into the economy or through grants to other levels of government, or (4) through the use of universal dividends (income)—in other words, "humanity credits"—as machines, computers, robots, and artificial intelligence take over an increasing number of jobs.

In the first interval (T), a publicly owned central bank participating with a state, county, or municipal bank, or a subsidiary of such, creates a loan of $100, which increases the money supply by $100. No interest or fees are charged, so there is no inflationary pressure on the goods and/or services created from the loan. The base money that the central bank spends into circulation to pay for the banking overhead would be figured as part of the overall growth or shrinkage of the economy, depending on the size of the workforce and the value of the goods and services in circulation.

When the loan is repaid, the money supply is reduced by $100 for a net gain/loss of zero. The money supply may be further altered by increasing or decreasing the rate at which loans are being created, based on the aforementioned amalgamated local price indices or, as noted, via tax rates and/or grants.

As long as the money supply expands or contracts proportionately to the availability of goods and services in circulation, prices will neither inflate nor deflate. The tax rate could be set to zero, if there is no inflation, or if there were deflation. In the latter case, additional government spending (base money) would be called for, or more local credit could be made available. So, instead of the fake quantitative easing (QE) enacted by the Fed following the 2008 crash—where the money went to the "too big to fail" banks to buy up defaulted collateralized assets at fire sale prices—in a public banking system, QE would be channeled directly into the economy, particularly via small businesses (which generated half the jobs in the U.S., before the 2008 crash).

Also, states, counties, municipalities, and other political subdivisions, would have the option of issuing zero-interest bonds, which could then be purchased by the central bank or the state bank, depending on whether the issuer of the bonds was the state, or a county or city. The proceeds from the bonds would be spent, by the party issuing the bonds, into the money supply. The repayment of the bonds would later be extracted from the money supply in the form of tax revenues or fees and then paid back to the public bondholder. The net effect of the bonds on the money supply is zero. Thus, bonds—at the state, county, municipal or other political subdivision level—are another means of temporarily adjusting the money supply and regulating the value of currency, as per inflationary or deflationary trends indicated by the LPI. The projects that could be funded are endless at this point, given the environmental destruction and infrastructure deterioration that has transpired under the final vulture stages of capitalism.

If the Central Bank and the entire network of state and local banks were publicly owned and did not charge interest, then the banks and their corresponding governments, working in concert, could thus maintain a sustainable economy and stable currency. Such a system was proposed in Greece[219], during the recent crisis, as the only viable solution to debt as an instrument of war and terrorism, before the eventual sellout of Greece by Syriza leader Alexis Tsipras, after the people voted "No!" to the plan which he accepted later from the cartel.

Given the starkly different outcomes of these models—private versus public control over money creation—we must ask why we would allow private ownership over currency, with its poison pill of usury, to doom the planet to economic tyranny, environmental destruction, the gutting

[219] http://www.truth-out.org/news/item/30852-dimitris-kazakis-syriza-has-no-plan-b-left-came-to-continue-with-austerity

of the value of labor, the legalization of the theft of assets, and a totalitarian society? The answer to this should be that we have no intention of allowing this to continue and that, as Jefferson said:

> "... I have sworn upon the altar of god eternal hostility against every form of tyranny over the mind of man." —from a letter to Dr. Benjamin Rush, September 23, 1800, later carved in stone as the inscription under the dome of the Jefferson Memorial, Washington, DC.

How nations, states, counties, and cities can solve their budget crises: Own a bank

As Jefferson, Madison, and Jackson learned (and as we've just underscored), privately controlled central banks are not businesses, but instruments of war and theft. Hamilton, who is now being promoted on Broadway and across the nation by financial interests in New York, sold the fledgling United States of America back to the British banks, whose mercenaries the colonial army (with the help of the French) had just defeated. This is treason.

The Revolutionary War against the cartel continues today. The poisonous recipe—austerity, budget deficits, spending cuts, sequestering, sale of public assets, and increased taxation—are unnecessary and devious solutions proposed by private banking interests and their corporate and government appointees (including "elected officials"[220]). The nations', states', counties', and cities' budget crises did not arise from too much spending or too little taxation. They arose because the world's largest banks, on Wall Street and in the City of London, manipulated the financial markets, particularly derivatives, as they froze credit to choke the money supply.

---

[220] More on this in *Step 5*.

This strategy on the part of the world's most powerful banks has been going on for centuries. Now, it's up to the public to take back control of the nation's money supply, thereby restoring U.S. sovereignty, and subsequently to provide credit and infuse currency into the local, state, regional, and national economies, while repairing the ubiquitous damage done by the Robber Barons.

How?

The Federal Reserve could provide a stimulus in the same way that it provided over $16 trillion in liquidity and short-term loans (between December 2007 and July 2010) to the "too big to fail" banks that own it.[221] (At that time, this was more money than the entire U.S. debt accumulated over the previous 241 years.) But the Fed has no intention of doing this—not because it would be too costly (the total deficit of all the states comes to less than 2% of the credit advanced for the bailout of the rapacious banks)—but because it is not part of the Fed's legal mandate, or so they claim. More honestly, the financiers who own the Fed use the central bank's control over Federal Reserve Notes (which they misbrand as U.S. dollars) to alternately inflate and choke the money supply and thereby acquire the 99%'s hard-earned assets. So, for starters, the Fed must be nationalized. This is the *sine qua non* of sovereignty.

In addition, any state or local policymaker truly interested in repairing the situation, including increasing lending, particularly to small businesses, the hardest hit by the credit squeeze, must consider the creation of an institution modeled on the Bank of North Dakota (BND)—currently the only state-owned bank in the country—and many of the original 13 colonies, which owned their own banks. The

---

[221] U.S. General Accounting Office, "Federal Reserve System: Opportunities Exist to Strengthen Policies and Processes for Managing Emergency Assistance," July 2011, p. 131.

BND has a 99-year history of safe, secure, and highly profitable banking in the public interest. North Dakota has the lowest unemployment and foreclosure rates in the country; and, during the orchestrated 2008 crash, while other states were foundering, had the largest budget surplus in its history. The private banks and their apologists will try to convince you this was due to the oil boom, but the Bakken oil fields are a recent development (2008), and one that is proving, ecologically and socially, to be more a boondoggle than a boon.

Since 2010, more than 20 states have introduced bills either to form state-owned banks or to do feasibility studies to determine the potential of publicly owned banks. A growing number of cities and counties are also considering such an initiative. Publicly owned banks are a win-win for the 99.999999%. Objections are usually based on misconceptions or lack of information.

A publicly owned bank, based on the BND model:

1. Generates new revenues for cities, counties, and states, directly through transfers of publicly owned bank surpluses (profits on loans [in the absence of a publicly owned central bank]) into the general fund, and indirectly by creating jobs and spurring local economic growth.

2. Lowers interest costs for governments. Public banks have access to low-cost funds from the Federal Reserve System and various government programs. The banks can pass savings on to the local governments that own them, when they finance infrastructure repair, replacement, or creation. The banks also may provide Letters of Credit to underwrite tax-exempt bonds at lower interest rates; or, help a city, county, or state issue a new bond at an interest rate lower than it could negotiate on the open market; or, buy bonds already issued and traded on the bond market, with interest payments then diverted to the city, county, or state, cutting costs by 40 to 50% (via reduction of interest charges on long-term capital investments, such as infrastructure and buildings).

3. Builds small businesses. In markets increasingly dominated by large corporations and the banks that own them, public banks provide essential lending to small businesses, to keep them competitive. Private banks have purposefully cut credit lines and loans to small businesses, driving many small businesses owners to use their credit cards (at much higher interest rates) or to go out of business.

4. Stabilizes local independent banks. In North Dakota, the BND serves the role of a mini-Fed, providing correspondent banking services to virtually every financial institution in North Dakota (including a Federal Funds program with daily volume of $330 million), check clearing, cash management services, and automated clearing house services. However, in most states, the independent bank associations have been hijacked by the large commercial and investment banks, so they oppose public banks.

5. Remains independent of private banking and corporate interests. Although the BND is a member of the Minneapolis Federal Reserve Bank, it is insured by the "full faith and credit" of North Dakota, not the privately controlled FDIC. This avoids unnecessary risk and expense, since the BND's chief depositor is the state, and the state's accounts are significantly larger than $250,000, the maximum covered by FDIC insurance.

6. Provides accountability, transparency, and prudent risk management. Publicly owned bank employees do not receive bonuses for short-term profits and speculative investments, in contrast to the "too big to fail" banks, which thrive on such recklessness (since they own the Fed and bail themselves out after each self-inflicted bankruptcy).

7. Creates new jobs and spurs economic growth. According to a 2010 study by the Center for State Innovation, if Washington State had a fully-operational publicly owned bank capitalized at $100 million during the 2008 recession, it would have supported $2.6 billion in new lending and helped to create 8,212 new small business jobs. Likewise, a proposed Oregon state bank would have helped local community banks expand lending by $1.3 billion and help small business create 5,391 new Oregon jobs in its first three to five years.

8. Is self-funding and self-sustaining. The BND keeps federally-guaranteed funds in the state and uses the profits on these to build a capital surplus from which loans are made to local businesses. Last we looked, the BND had a return on equity of 25-26% and contributed over $300 million to the state (its only shareholder) in the past decade—a notable achievement for a state with a population of approximately 750,000.

9. Keeps local money on Main Street—partnering with community banks by leveraging public funds into credit for local purposes. These are funds that would otherwise leave the state via Wall Street branch banks and be leveraged abroad, creating economic multipliers and jobs elsewhere.

10. Strengthens local banks by acting as a counter-cyclical ballast during periods when the private banks are choking the money supply,[222] thus easing credit shortfalls and preserving competition in local credit markets. There have been no bank failures in North Dakota during the ongoing financial crisis. By purchasing local bank stock, partnering with local banks on large loans, and providing other support, state and other publicly owned banks strengthen independent banks.

11. Stops the theft of public resources. The major central banks and

---

[222] https://popularresistance.org/federal-bank-regulator-drops-a-bombshell-as-corporate-media-snoozes/

the largest commercial and investment banks own most of the key corporations at the core of the global economy[223] as well as the most powerful governments (including their intelligence services and armed forces), acquired via control of the central bank[224] and its currency printing press. These banks (via their proxy governments) are not only attacking and destroying all nations that control their own banking and currency[225] (Afghanistan, Iraq, Iran, Libya, Syria, Tunisia, North Korea, etc.), but (after choking the money supply and destroying tax bases) are privatizing governments, in other words: profiteering in virtually all aspects of life, including armaments, medicine and drugs, insurance, education, housing, media, and food.

All key financial markets are now controlled and rigged by the financiers at the top of the system. Even foreign currency, stocks, bonds, and commodities markets are rigged.[226] Not satisfied with their pirates' booty, they are now prepared to steal money from depositors.[227] Clearly, public monies (taxes and fees, etc.) should be deposited in public banks, which operate in the public interest. It is the only way for states, counties, cities, and other governmental bodies to survive in a nation whose central bank is privately owned, and operated for the purpose of profiteering at the expense of the taxpayers.

Given the clear advantages of public banks, and their success record—

---

[223] www.newscientist.com/article/mg21228354.500-revealed--the-capitalist-network-that-runs-the-world.html

[224] http://www.scribd.com/doc/46627723/Federal-Reserve-Directors-A-Study-of-Corporate-and-Banking-Influence-Staff-Report-Committee-on-Banking-Currency-and-Housing-House-of-Representative coupled with http://www.scribd.com/doc/12866710/The-ownership-of-the-Federal-Reserve-as-exposed-by-Congressional-Committee-1976

[225] http://www.activistpost.com/2012/09/state-owned-central-banks-are-real.html

[226] http://coloradopublicbanking.blogspot.com/2015/02/the-running-tab-on-bank-fraud.html

[227] http://www.maxkeiser.com/2013/04/bail-out-is-out-bail-in-is-in-time-for-some-publicly-owned-banks/

despite the efforts of the private banking cartel to destroy them—what political and economic strategies should be employed in the U.S. to restore sovereignty and economic health?

Equality for debt slaves is not freedom

As we've noted, most of the money in the world is controlled by a small group of people, through their privately held, closely held, and public holding companies and the central banks which they operate. This control over the unaudited money creation process has enabled them to manipulate markets and buy key assets (governments, corporations, real estate, and natural resources) with impunity, as well as use a variety of overt and covert weapons to attack any threat to their hegemony over the planet.

The question of how the 99.999999% can remove this seemingly monolithic edifice of power is a subject of much debate, which, for starters, requires us to get past the illusion of political parties (Democrats, Republicans, Labour, Tories, etc.) as being entities distinct from the banks and corporations that control them. The maintenance of this illusion is mostly dependent on the belief that the "loss leaders" offered by each party make them distinct brands. For example, as previously noted, the come-on for the Democrats is "equality," meaning that we are all equal regardless of race, gender, religion, intelligence, etc. All this is well and good, except that, in the context of a small group of people controlling the world's currencies, economies, governments, religions, and media, what "equality" means is that we are equal debt slaves. In other words, the electorate confuses equality with freedom—a rather glaring logical fallacy.

Freedom is a different matter entirely. For us to be free, corporate control over the state (fascism) must be removed. What this involves, first and foremost, is the reintroduction of public control over money creation and regulation. Again, as Meyer Amschel Rothschild was

119

reputed to have said, "Give me control over a nation's money and I care not who makes the law."; vice versa, so it would be for the 99.999999%, as well. If we, the people, wish to have a democratic republic, then we, the people, must control our nation's money. It is the foundation of sovereignty, as prescribed in the U.S. Constitution (Article I, Sections 8 and 10): only Congress can create money.

In addition to a public banking network, there are two other requirements, after sovereign money, that are required for a democratic republic—verifiable voting and decentralized media—which we shall discuss in our next chapter, *Step 5—Restoring Democracy*.

Who advocates for sovereignty?

There are a number of monetary reform groups and political organizations in the U.S. that have proposed strategies for bringing about such a change. Here are the most compelling.

Let's begin with the Public Banking Institute (PBI), of which I was a founding board member.

How the Public Banking Institute sees money

The Public Banking Institute was organized as a result of the writings of Ellen Brown, particularly her book, *Web of Debt*, which rediscovered that L. Frank Baum's *The Wizard of Oz* was written as a monetary allegory. More importantly, the book also highlighted the proven operations of the now 99-year old Bank of North Dakota (BND).

Our kudos to Ellen Brown for bringing public banking to the public's attention. Among the many points that Brown has made is that public banking has been around a long time—millennia, in fact, going back at least to Sumeria. All the original 13 colonies created their own money and a few of them had their own bank. The Continental Congress also printed its own money, as did the U.S., briefly, under Presidents Lincoln and Kennedy.

If one looks at the history of colonial America and the United States of America, private control over money creation and central banking has logged just over 145 years, while other forms of money creation, including public banks without central banking, have logged 293 years (156 years as colonies and 137 years since the Declaration of Independence (minus forty years of the First and Second Banks of U.S.), ending in 1913, with the creation of the "Federal" Reserve System.

As we have emphasized, one of the central debates regarding money creation revolves around interest and its effect on monetary stability. Here are two quotes from Brown regarding this issue:

> "We actually need publicly owned banks for a capitalist market economy to run properly. Banking, money and credit are not market goods but are economic infrastructure, just as roads and bridges are physical infrastructure. By providing inexpensive, accessible financing to the free enterprise sector of the economy, public banks make commerce more vital and stable."
> —Ellen Brown, "Public Banks Are Key to Capitalism," *The New York Times*, October 2, 2013.[228]

> "If we had a financial system that returned the interest collected from the public directly to the public, 35 percent could be lopped off the price of everything we buy." —Ellen Brown, "It's the Interest, Stupid! Why Bankers Rule the World," *Truthout*, November 8, 2012.

---

[228] http://www.nytimes.com/roomfordebate/2013/10/01/should-states-operate-public-banks/public-banks-are-essential-to-capitalism

In the former article, Brown's statement that "We actually need publicly owned banks for a capitalist market economy to run properly," is self-contradictory, as we showed in *Step 1*: Capitalism is a system based on the primacy of capital, a commodity created when interest is charged on money-as-a unit-of-accounting for the value created by labor, thus turning money into a store of value, i.e., a commodity; on the other hand, public banking is a system that, ultimately, treats money as a public utility and unit of accounting. Certainly, public banks can make any economy more vital and stable, as we see in Germany and Switzerland, but trying to sell public banking because it is good for capitalism is disingenuous, much as saying G-d is good for devil worshipping. As we showed earlier in this chapter, as long as the central bank is privately owned, inflation and plutocracy remain and, contrary to Brown's claim, banking, money and credit will remain market goods.

In the latter article quoted above, after paying (unspoken) homage to the late Margrit Kennedy's work regarding the hidden costs of interest in everything we buy and sell, Brown's remedy is simply for public banks to charge interest and return the profits to the money supply. It sounds good, but such a system would still be inflationary, since it would add to the overhead of any business that takes out a loan; therefore, it would raise the costs of goods and services, and it would unnecessarily consolidate the power of false value in the hands of a government bank. No bank, public or private, should be injecting false value (that is, value that does not represent labor or its adjuncts [machines, computers, robots, and artificial intelligence]), because such false value requires real value to be taken out of the system to prevent runaway inflation, as we have seen via the actions of the privately owned Fed and the regular crashes it oversees, every five years or so, since it was created. During those contractions, false value (interest) steals real value through its call on collateralized assets, replacing the value created by labor.

For example, let's say I own an apple orchard and produce apples and apple sauce, and that my brand has an established and loyal customer base. At some point, I decide to borrow money from the public banking network to buy more land and expand my operation. All my interest payments will then become expenses, which will add to the price of my product, whether or not the interest income I pay to the banking system is 100% returned to the money supply; thus, there is an inflationary aspect to charging interest, even if you are a public bank returning all your interest income to the money supply. Besides, the BND does not return all of its interest income to the state's general fund; it keeps a large portion and leverages it to expand its loan portfolio. Granted, the BND must do this to achieve a profit (actually, since it operates as non-profit bank, profit, as a line item, is noted as a fund surplus).

In addition to its contribution to inflation, interest engenders the conflict of capital versus labor. Although Brown has long pointed out that the two principle ways in which money is employed are as a unit of accounting and as a store of value—and she has argued for the former as being the most stable form of money—she then turns around and argues that charging interest is okay, if it is done by a public bank, failing to see that the moment interest is charged, money changes from a unit of accounting (for our labor) into a store of value (capital). In that very instant, labor is devalued and turns into a commodity (human capital), leading to labor's debt enslavement and the eventual theft of the fruits of labor (the value it creates). This is why, after working their whole lives, most people have no assets to show for it—because the value they created has been stolen from them via interest and other casino tricks.

Granted, in a world where private and public banking exist side by side, usury and the use of faux legal tender (private bank notes, e.g., "Federal" Reserve Notes) are part and parcel of the economic, monetary, and political paradigm; but, in a world of public banking networks, private bank notes and usury are unnecessary and counter-productive, as we detailed in our models earlier in this chapter.

Additionally, like practitioners of Social Credit and Modern Monetary Theory, Brown is confused about the relationship between economic activity and accounting:

> "If [the Chinese] have some bad loans, they just write them off. Because nobody's hurt — nobody actually put up the money. The money was just created as an accounting entry, so you can write off those accounting entries if you need to, to save your economy. You don't need to force austerity on people who didn't do it, who weren't liable for it, who weren't at fault. We pretend like money is actually owed to someone, but it's not. It was created as credit on the books — it can be written off." — Ellen Brown, in a radio interview by Sarah Westhall on "Business Game Changers," 11/20/17

An accounting entry for a loan or grant is a record of economic activity, not the activity itself. As we have seen with the various accounting scandals, misrepresenting corporate facts on spreadsheets is easy to do, just like "the government's" economic reports. Thus, an accounting entry does not, as Brown claims, increase the money supply. That occurs when the credit to the borrower's account is spent into the economy.

While it is true that the Chinese were able to write off non-performing loans and grants that they issued, before they joined the WTO and were forced to do otherwise, this does not negate the fact that the money issued remained in the money supply, which becomes an inflationary pressure, since the project did not produce a commensurate amount of circulating goods and services. What negated this inflationary pressure were all the successful grants and loans, which increased the circulation of goods and services, as well as the velocity of money, in the Chinese economy. But since joining the WTO, many Chinese political subdivisions find themselves deeply in debt.

Ultimately, by promulgating such notions under Brown's leadership, PBI reduces the notion of public banking to a shadow of itself, wittingly or unwittingly ignoring the unique nature of publicly owned central banks, and thus reducing public banking to a partial solution, one cause among many, which it is not.

What the American Monetary Institute advocates

Another notable monetary reformer is Stephen Zarlenga, founder of the American Monetary Institute, upon whose work former Representative (D-OH) and Presidential candidate Dennis Kucinich's "The NEED Act" was based. In it, Mr. Zarlenga proposes the following:

"How The NEED Act Solves the Problem in 3 major steps:

"1) The Federal Reserve is incorporated into our government, where people think it is now. A new Monetary Authority is established to avoid both inflation and deflation.

"2) Simple accounting rule changes will prohibit banks from creating what we use for money by decisively ending fractional reserve lending. Banks would lend real money they have or receive from savers. This is what people think happens now.

"3) Government creates and spends new money into circulation for infrastructure, education and health care; starting with the $2.2 trillion the engineers say we need to make our infrastructure safe, over the next 5 years. This alone will create over 7 million good jobs quickly."[229]

---

[229] "Sequesters, Shutdowns and Defaults,"[229] *Huffington Post*, October, 11, 2013."

Both Brown and Zarlenga are proposing models that incorporate private banks charging interest, which, as demonstrated in our proof earlier in this chapter, would result in the same outcome as we have now: private control over money and nations; that is, the current power structure would not change. By control over money creation, we do not mean just control over central banking; loans with interest are another means to control money creation. And, of course, control over money creation creates political, economic, and military control. Thus, economics must be studied side-by-side with political science, to paint an accurate picture of the dynamics of power, as well as the production and distribution of goods and services.

Although Zarlenga's model requires that banks loan only what they possess, the interest on such loans necessarily injects false value (for which no labor has been performed) into the system. As long as private parties are allowed to profit from money creation and credit, they will end up owning the key assets[230] and resources, by which they will end up usurping sovereignty,[231] as we've noted (particularly in our example of a public central bank with private commercial banks charging interest, as Zarlenga is proposing). Ultimately, private banks will find a way around any regulation designed to prevent them from doing what they want,[232] as they have so amply demonstrated.

A new wrinkle in Zarlenga's plan is (in point #1) to create a Monetary Authority to avoid inflation and deflation. While we agree that having an agency to monitor the value of the currency is a good idea (we propose that the currency value should be measured [at a local level] relative to the cost of a basket of goods and services defined by a

---

[230] http://www.newscientist.com/article/mg21228354.500-revealed--the-capitalist-network-that-runs-the-world.html

[231] http://coloradopublicbanking.blogspot.com/2013/04/100-years-of-servitude.html

[232] http://dealbook.nytimes.com/2014/02/13/banks-in-london-devise-way-around-europes-bonus-rules/

constitutional amendment, the Economic Bill of Rights), Zarlenga's model necessarily creates inflationary factors (via the charging of interest).

Additionally, given the limited details that Zarlenga has provided, it is difficult to see how new money would be added to the system (to reflect the growing value of the circulating goods and services created by labor), other than by direct spending on the part of a public central bank or monetary authority, somewhat in the manner of Soviet central planning, which is an inefficient and inaccurate process, whether it is conducted under state capitalism (by the political elites), as in the case of the Soviets and the Chinese, or whether it is conducted as private socialism (by the economic elites), as in the case of the U.S.

This is not to diminish the importance of federal projects (highways, dams, airports, etc.), but there must be a process for the distribution of base money and no-interest credit to states, counties, and cities, as well as to the general public and business community, with due regard to inflationary and deflationary pressures (measured by the local price index [LPI]). This is particularly important as automation and robotic advancements are employed to eliminate jobs and shorten the work week, which are key elements in a sustainable economy operating under a progressive philosophy.

In other words, the monitoring of currency value, from market to market, is what should determine the availability of credit from local public banks, which would do so at no interest. As noted earlier in this chapter, creditworthiness would still be determined by the repayment of loans.

Finally, Zarlenga calls for "decisively ending fractional reserve lending," but as the Bank of England noted in 2014, this is not how banks make loans; rather, they make loans as they see fit and create reserves by borrowing from the central bank, which controls monetary policy and, thereby, economic activity. In Zarlenga's model, in which the Federal Reserve System would be nationalized (thank you), the Board of Governors would then control the availability of credit by adjusting the interest rate at which member banks would borrow. So, we come back around to private banks injecting false value into a commodified currency.

The platform and philosophy of the Green Party

Finally, let's look at a plan put forth by Dr. Jill Stein, the 2012 and 2016 Green Party Presidential candidate, which she calls "the Green New Deal."[233]

Stein incorporates many good ideas into her plan—including public banking, an economic bill of rights, verifiable voting, and media decentralization—but as is often the case with the platforms of political parties, and like Brown's and Zarlenga's plans, there is a great deal of inconsistency and conflicts in Stein's proposals; after all, traditional political parties operate on a model of being "all things to all people."

For example, in the section entitled Real Financial Reform, the Green New Deal says, "... democratize monetary policy to bring about public control of the money supply and credit creation," and "... support the formation of federal, state, and municipal public-owned banks that function as non-profit utilities." However, in the same section, the plan calls for breaking up the big banks (not eliminating them), using the FDIC to transform failed banks into public banks (the FDIC is a private corporation designed to transfer assets of failed private banks to other private banks), regulating derivatives (the casino would continue because usury would be maintained), and taxing the bonuses of

---

[233]

https://d3n8a8pro7vhmx.cloudfront.net/jillstein/pages/620/attachments/original/1344126365/Green_New_Deal_letter_size_printout.pdf

investment bankers (that is, the incentive to maintain rigged markets would continue). Which shall it be: public control of the money supply, or a competition between public banks and criminal private banks?

Again, as we show earlier in this chapter, a mix of public and private banking eventually leads to the same inflationary pressures and private control over the process that we have now.

In an interview with Laura Flanders on GritTV[234] (10/22/13), Stein continues in the same vein, stating that the Green New Deal would "reduce the deficit by creating jobs and jump starting the American economy." (11:43—11:47) Either Stein believes that telling the American people the truth—that private control over central bank money creation necessarily creates an ever-increasing national debt—would be too overwhelming for them (so, she talks about debt reduction), or she herself does not have an accurate picture of the power structure and, instead, believes that the traditional political party prescription of consolidating various interest groups (by promising jobs and economic growth) is the only viable way to counter a system dominated by what she calls "Wall Street interests." Wall Street and the City of London are not interest groups; they control the planetary power pyramid. They are a criminal cartel.

To her credit, Stein is tireless in her efforts to rouse the public to the issues that threaten our very existence; yet, we cannot help but wonder what purpose is served by not facing the facts: an international cartel of central bankers owns and controls the key currencies, markets, corporations, governments, armed services, intelligence services, voting processes, and media outlets. Until control over money creation and credit regulation is returned IN ITS ENTIRETY to the public sector, the world will remain at the mercy of merciless usurers who aim to "reduce the surplus population"—as Charles Dickens so forcefully

---

[234] http://www.youtube.com/watch?v=nm7vThOD0G0

put it via Ebenezer Scrooge, usurer from the City of London, in *A Christmas Carol*—to approximately 1/14 its current size, by any means necessary, including: war and the poisoning of our air, water, land, food, and medicines; as well as, the purposeful denial of social safety nets, including healthcare and food stamps, while they choke the money supply to increase bankruptcies, foreclosures, and homelessness.

Not understanding the root cause of global dysfunction—and failing to put it front and center of any transformative movement—results in a strategy of "old politics," trying to romance each interest group on their own terms, and scattering the energy of the movement. This is a disservice, because it presumes folks aren't capable of seeing outside of their own self-interest, and because of the piecemeal analysis that it offers, with its old-world, Keynesian message of reducing military spending to pay for needed social services.

War is created by the banks for: profit (the theft of resources and labor), power (the theft of sovereignty), and population reduction (the theft of life). Such thoughts and choices would be obsolete in a system of public banking, verifiable voting, and decentralized media. A truly transformative system would serve people, not capital. With a public banking network, a far-reaching set of universal social programs (income, healthcare, education, etc.) costs a pittance compared with the cost of war, health, and education profiteering under a privately controlled system; and, in a public banking network, no debt would be accumulated.

While Stein understands that present planetary circumstances require an economic and ecologic transformation, she does not speak of the spiritual requirements for such a shift in focus (from capital to people), apparently believing it would be an anathema to winning over the public's good will, thereby failing to meet one of the threshold requirements for the change she desperately seeks (i.e., personal and societal evolution). Yet, despite this inconsistency, she knows that extraordinary times demand extraordinary actions, and that the key is in numbers of people: "It's time for all of us to stand up together, maybe on the same day, and show how powerful this movement ... is." (13:33-13:42) Amen to that, sister!

And that is exactly what we have learned in our efforts to bring public banking legislation to bear in over 20 states and various cities: Given the stranglehold that the international criminal bankers have over nations and states, we need to show up *en masse* at county seats and municipal buildings, look our "representatives" in the eye and ask them: "Which side are you on, the banks or the people?

Bernie Sanders: Capitalism with a "democratic socialist" twist

Finally, we witnessed the unexpected Presidential candidacy of Senator Bernie Sanders (I-VT), who, over the years, has proposed a number of monetary reforms, including an audit of the Federal Reserve System and, during his 2016 campaign for the Presidential nomination of the Democratic Party, "breaking up the big banks" and reinstating the Glass-Steagall Act.

Where have we seen "breaking up the big banks" before? With the trustbusters, back in Teddy Roosevelt's day, when the focus was on breaking up Standard Oil. And what became of that?

While the public was led to believe that the Rockefellers' monopolistic control over oil and petroleum in the U.S. was broken, in fact, when the U.S. forced, via anti-trust litigation, Standard Oil to split up, it created 34 separate companies, in all of which John D. Rockefeller still owned significant equity.

Breaking up the big banks would not be any different. It would not change the fact that a few families control money creation. The same goes for Glass-Steagall; when it was in effect, it did nothing to change the power structure. So, while we agree in principle with many of the social programs that Sanders proposes, at least at a generic level, their implementation and budgetary efficiency are only possible when the people of the United States of America regain sovereignty by nationalizing their central bank.

Given the demise of a long list of politicians—including Presidents and Congressmen—that have challenged the Federal Reserve, Sanders' circumspection in this regard—i.e., only going so far as to suggest the "too big to fail banks" must be downsized and that the separation of commercial and investment banking must be reinstated—may be seen, with some generosity, given certain *sub rosa* "pressures" exerted upon him, as "discretion is the greater part of valor."

So, regardless of the hacked outcome of Sanders and the people versus a rigged electoral system (including the dirty tricks of the "Democratic" Party cabal, as proven by the leaked emails posted to Wikileaks, and the murder of Seth Rich, who provided them), regardless of the five swing states hacked for Trump, and regardless of a mass media that intentionally distorts the strength of the progressive movement, we see once again that there are millions of people willing to vote with their feet. As noted by Dr. Stein, the growth of those willing to do this will be a key factor in bringing a tipping point that results in a progressive outcome.

STEP 5—RESTORING DEMOCRACY

"I have sworn upon the altar of God, eternal hostility against every form of tyranny over the mind of man."
—Thomas Jefferson, in a letter to Dr. Benjamin Rush, September 23, 1800

Modern history is a cartel-sponsored myth

While public banking is the *sine qua non* of sovereignty, followed by verifiable voting and decentralized media, there are other necessary requisites, beginning with our ability to rediscover and learn from our own history.

We're taught in school that the United States began as a unique experiment in laissez-faire capitalism and participatory democracy, but this is pure mythology.

By the time North America was colonized, private banking interests were largely in control of Europe, including Britain and, by default, its 13 American colonies. When the British bankers discovered—by way of Benjamin Franklin's testimony before Parliament—that the colonies printed their own money and that this practice was largely responsible for the low incidence of poverty in the colonies, they ordered Parliament to ban paper currencies in the colonies. This is corroborated by Franklin's later testimony that cites this prohibition against local script as one of the chief grievances of the colonists.

Given the pointed and well-funded Orwellian efforts of the international banking cartel to destroy any documentation that potentially undermines their hegemony over money creation, it has become difficult to determine the genuineness of certain quotes attributed to various American revolutionaries and other key historical figures regarding their views on money and banking; but, it is clear from the comments and actions of the founders that the prohibition of the colonies printing their own currency caused a rapid shrinking of the money supply and a depression, and, in turn, became a *cause célèbre* for revolution.

Founders foundered in money matters

Yet, despite their adherence to paper currency, the nation's founders did not fully grasp how money works and how the European usurers leveraged privately controlled money creation to gain control over corporations and governments. So, despite defeating the British bankers' Hessian mercenaries during the Revolutionary War, President Washington ignored Jefferson's objections and decided in favor of Alexander Hamilton's proposal to create the First Bank of the United States, which was modeled on and controlled by the Bank of England, a private central bank. Thus, the criminal bankers once again gained power over their former colonies, essentially usurping the short-lived sovereignty of the United States.

> "And I sincerely believe, with you, that banking establishments are more dangerous than standing armies; and that the principle of spending money to be paid by posterity, under the name of funding, is but swindling futurity on a large scale." —Letter from Thomas Jefferson to John Taylor, May 28,1816 (10:31), from the Monticello archives

> "Bank-paper must be suppressed, and the circulating medium must be restored to the nation to whom it belongs." —Letter from Thomas Jefferson to John Wayles Eppes, September 11, 1813 (PTJ:RS, 6:494), from the Monticello archives

Although a series of Presidents and other public officials resisted the cartel's aggressions, private control over money creation endured and proved to be the bankers' lynchpin to power, enabling a handful of families to gain control over the key central banks, commercial and investment banks, corporations, and governments of the world.[235]

President Madison's refusal to renew the 20-year charter of the First Bank of the United States in 1811 brought reprisals from cartel-controlled Britain, forcing a declaration of war by the U.S. Shortly thereafter, the British bankers used British naval operations to sucker the U.S. into further debt, resulting in the misguided establishment of the Second Bank of the U.S., another shill for British and European bankers.

Debt as a weapon of mass destruction

President Andrew Jackson refused to renew the charter of the Second Bank of the U.S., thus precipitating a depression as threatened by Nicholas Biddle, who headed up the bank for the European parties that controlled it. Seven unsuccessful attempts were made on Jackson's life following his stand.

> "More than eight millions of the stock of this bank are held by foreigners ... is there no danger to our liberty and independence in a bank that in its nature has so little to bind it to our country? ... Controlling our currency, receiving our public moneys, and holding thousands of our citizens in dependence ... would be more formidable and dangerous than a military power of the enemy." —Andrew Jackson, July 1832, in his veto message to Congress,

---

[235] http://www.newscientist.com/article/mg21228354.500-revealed--the-capitalist-network-that-runs-the-world.html and https://www.scribd.com/document/12866710/The-ownership-of-the-Federal-Reserve-as-exposed-by-Congressional-Committee-1976

"I have had men watching you for a long time and I am convinced that you have used the funds of the bank to speculate in the breadstuffs of the country. When you won, you divided the profits amongst you, and when you lost, you charged it to the Bank. ... You are a den of vipers and thieves." —Andrew Jackson, 1834, on closing the Second Bank of the U.S.

Following Jackson's successful resistance, the banking cartel sought to drive the U.S. into debt via public works projects. After the very successful Erie Canal project, financed by bonds, a number of copycat public works projects were begun, primarily for canals and railroads.

In the decade running from 1820 to 1830, state governments had borrowed a total of just twenty-six million dollars. In the next five years, new borrowing rose to forty million dollars. And in the next three years—1836 to 1838—borrowing exceeded one hundred million dollars. In a very short period, American states had accumulated obligations roughly equal to the combined national debt of Russia, Prussia, and the Netherlands.[236]

This strategy, of forcing nations into debt, has been employed worldwide by the banking cartel for centuries; for example, with the Suez Canal, in Egypt.[237]

Assassinating presidents; creating wars; and destroying sovereignty

The Anglo-European bankers and their U.S. partners continued to press for another privately owned and operated national bank. When

---

[236] Alasdair Roberts, *America's First Great Depression: Economic Crisis and Political Disorder after the Panic of 1837*, Cornell University Press, 2012, pp. 51-52, 63-66.

[237] http://www.delanceyplace.com/view-archives.php?p=2829

President Zachary Taylor made known his intention in 1850 to block any attempt at such a bank,[238] he was poisoned.

Fearing that the United States would remain sovereign, issue its own currency, and put them out of business, the banking cartel exacerbated the divisions between North and South, helped finance the Confederacy,[239] and attempted to drive the U.S. into debt in order to fund the Union Army. At that point, President Lincoln was told by Wall Street that they would lend him the funds to fight the war—at 24 to 36% interest!

> "I see in the near future a crisis approaching that unnerves me and causes me to tremble for the safety of my country ... corporations have been enthroned and an era of corruption in high places will follow, and the money power of the country will endeavor to prolong its reign by working upon the prejudices of the people until all wealth is aggregated in a few hands and the Republic is destroyed." —President Abraham Lincoln, November 21, 1864, in a letter to Col. William F. Elkins, *The Lincoln Encyclopedia*, Archer H. Shaw, Macmillan, New York, 1950.

Lincoln, whose career is filled speeches and letters in support of a government-issued national currency, refused to capitulate to the usurers, choosing instead to implement the Constitutional provisions of Article I, Section 8, to print real U.S. dollars (Greenbacks) to pay for

---

[238] The idea of a national bank "is dead, and will not be revived in my time." Michael F. Holt, *The Rise and Fall of the American Whig Party: Jacksonian Politics and the Onset of the Civil War.* Oxford University Press, 1999, p. 272.

[239] Louisiana Senator Judah P. Benjamin, QC (Queen's counsel), was an English agent, and Confederate cabinet member, doing the bidding of the banking cartel that controlled Britain.

the war. This was the cartel's worst nightmare. As the *London Times* noted:

> "If this mischievous financial policy, which has its origin in North America, shall become endurated down to a fixture, then that Government will furnish its own money without cost. It will pay off debts and be without debt. It will have all the money necessary to carry on its commerce. It will become prosperous without precedent in the history of the world. The brains, and wealth of all countries will go to North America. That country must be destroyed or it will destroy every monarchy on the globe." —Hazard Circular, *London Times*, 1865

Previous to this clever piece of propaganda, the cartel had exerted control over the ever-corrupt U.S. Congress, which passed the National Banking Acts of 1863 and 1864, essentially forcing the U.S. government to issue treasury bonds, on which principal and interest must be paid, to receive the usurers' private bank notes, rather than to continue issuing debt-free Greenbacks. Once again, sovereignty of the U.S. government had been usurped by the Anglo-Euro-American banking cartel.

Selling the snake oil of "sound money" and the golden calf

Lincoln—who was hoping to reverse the National Banking Acts and thwart the cartel's move to reinstate the gold standard and choke the money supply—was assassinated.[240] By 1866, the cartel's relentless murderous methods and bribes in pursuit of power managed to re-

---

[240] A detailed reading of the testimony at the trial of the conspirators indicates that the banking cartel was behind the assassination. Gerald G. McGeer, *The Conquest of Poverty*, Chapter V, "Lincoln, the Practical Economist," The Garden City Press, Gardenvale, Quebec, 1935.

establish the gold standard, causing a drastic shrinking of the money supply and depression throughout the land, which continued to get worse. By 1871, riots broke out across the country, with many voters calling for the use of Greenbacks and silver.

The bankers clearly felt threatened, and responded with even more severe measures, including the demonetization of silver in 1873 and the use of loans as blackmail, as evidenced in this letter distributed to all members of the American Bankers Association:

> "It is advisable to do all in your power to sustain such prominent daily and weekly newspapers, especially the Agricultural and Religious Press, as will oppose the greenback issue of paper money and that you will also withhold patronage from all applicants who are not willing to oppose the government issue of money. To repeal the Act creating bank notes, or to restore to circulation the government issue of money will be to provide the people with money and will therefore seriously affect our individual profits as bankers and lenders. See your congressman at once and engage him to support our interest that we may control legislation." —James Buel, Secretary, American Bankers Association, 1877

Using the ruse of "sound money," that is, currency supposedly backed by gold, the bankers continued to alternately expand and choke the money supply and steal the assets built by labor.

Plutocrats arrogantly declare their intentions

In the age of the Robber Barons, arrogance was fashionable and forthcoming, revealing their true intentions:

> "On Sept 1st, 1894, we will not renew our loans under any consideration. On Sept 1st, we will demand our money. We will

140

foreclose and become mortgagees in possession. We can take two-thirds of the farms west of the Mississippi, and thousands of them east of the Mississippi as well, at our own price ... Then the farmers will become tenants as in England ..." —1891, American Bankers Association, as printed in the *Congressional Record* of April 29, 1913

In the throes of this criminal scam, William Jennings Bryan, the Democratic candidate for President in 1896, sought to loosen the bankers grip on money creation by re-monetizing silver:

"We will answer their demand for a gold standard by saying to them: You shall not press down upon the brow of labor this crown of thorns, you shall not crucify mankind upon a cross of gold."

Part of the bankers' strategy against Bryan was to instruct factory bosses to tell their workers that the business would shut down and everyone would lose their jobs if Bryan was elected. Bryan was narrowly defeated and ran again in 1900 and 1908, also coming up short.

The false flag of economic depression once again provides an excuse

The next major orchestrated contraction was in 1907, with the central bankers, behind J.P. Morgan, printing $200 million to loan to the illiquid banks. Woodrow Wilson was fooled just like most Americans:

"All this trouble could be averted if we appointed a committee of six or seven men like J.P. Morgan to handle the affairs of our country."[241]

Not everyone fell for the scam:

> "Those not favorable to the money trust could be squeezed out of business and the people frightened into demanding changes in the banking and currency laws which the Money Trust would frame." —Rep. Charles A. Lindbergh (R-MN)[242]

Nevertheless, on December 23rd, 1913, with a significant share of Congress already in recess, the Senate passed the Federal Reserve Act via a technicality (the Senate had not properly adjourned). Despite this, Wilson signed the act, over the objections of a few brave men:

> "The financial system has been turned over to ... the federal reserve board. That board administers the finance system by authority of ... a purely profiteering group. The system is private, conducted for the sole purpose of obtaining the greatest possible profits from the use of other people's money." —Rep Charles A, Lindbergh (R-MN)

> "We have in this country one of the most corrupt institutions the world has ever known. I refer to the Federal Reserve Board ... This evil institution has impoverished ... the people of the United States ... and has practically bankrupted our Government. It has done this through ... the corrupt practice of the moneyed vultures who control it." —Rep. Louis T, McFadden (R-PA)

---

[241] H.S. Kenan, *The Federal Reserve Bank* [Los Angeles: The Noontide Press, 1968, p. 105.

[242] Charles A. Lindbergh, *Banking and Currency and the Money Trust*, National Capital Press, Inc., 1913.

Wilson later regretted his actions:

> "I am a most unhappy man. I have unwittingly ruined my country. A great industrial nation is now controlled by its system of credit. We are no longer a government by free opinion, no longer a government by conviction and the vote of the majority, but a government by the opinion and duress of a small group of dominant men." —Woodrow Wilson, 1919[243]

The printing press that bought the world

It's been all downhill for democracy ever since, with the Federal Reserve System acting as a backstop for the cartel's U.S. and foreign[244] commercial and investment banks, and their corporations, as they plunder the planet.

The result of this consolidation of power[245]—over money creation, transnational corporations (including the mass media and voting machines) and government—is, by definition, a fascist system; that is, corporate control over the state, capital over labor, and criminality over law.

As we have demonstrated, this power is a result of private control over money creation and, despite the manipulation of laws and control of massive armaments—including top secret electronic, chemical, and biologic weaponry capable of geological, meteorological, and biological warfare—the cartel's power remains dependent on its dominion over money. Without it, it could not bribe and bully the

---

[243] *The American Mercury*, George Jean Nathan and H.L. Mencken, 1924, p. 56.

[244] Federal Reserve Notes became the world's reserve currency in a few short years following the blueprint adopted during a conclave of representatives of the Allied forces at Bretton Woods, New Hampshire, in 1944.

[245] www.newscientist.com/article/mg21228354.500-revealed--the-capitalist-network-that-runs-the-world.html

various levels of government (federal, state, county, and municipal), the military, the police, and its hitmen to serve at its will.

The *sine qua non* of democracy

Also, as we have detailed, there is an antidote for private control over money creation, which is, obviously, public control over money creation. Indeed, this has been the battle, particularly over the past five centuries, beginning in Europe, expanding to North America, and then the rest of the world: private versus public banking.

Understanding the difference is simple. Economics, stripped of obfuscation invented by the usurers to obscure their crimes, is not rocket science. Anyone with an elementary understanding of mathematics knows that money accumulates faster if one reinvests it rather than giving it away to those who use it in their personal interest, speculate with it, spend it on luxuries, and leverage it to subjugate others. Public banking is simply a means of leveraging taxpayer dollars in the public interest. It's been practiced longer than private banking and—left to its own devices, unfettered by the private cartel's assassins, counterfeiters, speculators, *agent provocateurs*, mercenaries, and lackeys—has shown its fiscal superiority on virtually every continent and in every age, including implementation by the original 13 American colonies, the Continental Congress, and during the Lincoln presidency.

This does not mean that, in and of itself, public banking is sufficient to restore democracy. The use of public banking by Hitler and Stalin, though effective in accumulating capital and driving economic growth, shows that public banking alone is not enough to guarantee a just and progressive society; but, as we've shown, a public banking network is a proven way to create a stable currency and—if coupled with verifiable voting and decentralized media—is a proven way to create a democratic economy and republic.

Federal, state, and many local governments are cartel owned and operated

As noted, late in the first decade of the 21st Century, a public banking movement resurfaced in the United States. Since 2010, bills to study public banking or implement a public bank have entered the legislative process from bi-partisan sources in over 20 states and, in turn, germinating initiatives at the county and city[246] level. Even the U.S. Congress has faced bi-partisan bills to nationalize the Federal Reserve, from Rep. Dennis Kucinich, D-OH (National Emergency Employment Defense [NEED] Act of 2011), and audit the Federal Reserve, from Rep. Ron Paul, R-TX (Federal Reserve Sunshine Act of 2009) and Sen. Bernie Saunders, I-VT (Federal Reserve Transparency Act of 2009).

It is a testament to the ubiquitous power of the banking cartel that no matter how far along any of these efforts make it through the legislative process, the cartel always has a means to prevent implementation; for example, in 2011 when both branches of the California legislature approved a measure (AB 750) to study a public bank and Gov. Jerry Brown, a so-called "liberal," vetoed it.

In Colorado, from 2012 through 2014, Colorado Public Banking brought four different initiatives, back-to-back-to-back-to-back, for a ballot measure regarding a publicly owned state bank. Over the course of these initiatives, the legislative, executive, and judicial branches of the state government all made clear their disdain for the bill and refused to permit the electorate to vote on it. Not content with stopping the electorate from considering these measures, the cartel's red and blue political brands within Colorado have sought further limitations on

---

[246] On April 26, 2017, the Santa Fe City Council voted unanimously to create a Public Banking Task Force to study the issue. Other cities and states now considering similar measures include San Francisco, Santa Rosa (CA), Oakland, Berkeley, Philadelphia, Pittsburgh, Seattle, St. Louis, New Jersey, Washington, and Alaska.

initiatives, beginning with greater signature requirements, as well as limiting subject matters, so that holistically related issues cannot be dealt with in the same initiative,[247] clearly revealing the domestic and foreign interests to whom these traitors pay obeisance.

All politics are local

Again, if the public is going to take back control over money creation and regulation—and use it as a means of accounting for and supporting its own labor, rather than as a commodity to devalue its labor—then this movement must begin in the U.S. at the city and county level, where folks can go down to the municipal building or county courthouse, look their so-called representatives in the eye, and ask them, "Which side are you on, the banks or the people?" Even as the cartel attempts to thwart such basic community organizing, there have been some successes.[248]

Of course, there are more facets to creating a people-oriented system than just control over money creation. As we have noted, by leveraging the money and credit system, the international banking cartel controls almost all key corporations, governments, and natural resources; but, there remains much that is still in play that could begin to turn around this depraved state of affairs, including local public banks, power generation, food, health care, and education—as long as we remain clear that the root cause of global dysfunction is private control over money creation, and that we tie back each initiative to this primary issue. To scatter our energies on projects that will not change control over money creation is to dilute our ability to effect change, which is

---

[247] http://www.denverpost.com/2016/11/08/colorado-amendment-71-constitutional-amendments-election-results/

[248] http://inthesetimes.com/rural-america/entry/18976/thomas-linzey-interview-on-corporate-control-and-community-rights and http://celdf.org/2016/03/press-release-colorado-supreme-court-rules-local-self-government-state-constitutional-amendment-can-advance-to-next-stage-toward-ballot/

one of the strategies that the cartel uses to waste our time, with various organizations and movements whose misdirection they control or simply support.

Just as we have seen at the federal and state level, many of the statutory local laws on the books were written by the cartel to secure their monopoly over money creation, thus it may be necessary, where possible, to re-write local laws through the adoption of a home rule charter or through ballot amendments, where such options have not been eliminated by puppet legislatures and rigged voting machines. Here, too, just as in the TPP trade agreement that keeps reappearing in different forms, the cartel will claim that corporate courts supersede federal courts, just as it seeks to use its control over states to override the will of the people at the local level.[249]

This is an old constitutional battle of centralized (federal) power versus decentralized (state and local) sovereignty. The replacement of the Articles of Confederation by the Constitution was a victory for the federalists, as well as the central bankers, who prefer corralling small groups of decision makers and providing them expanded powers.

> "It is difficult to get a man to understand something, when his salary depends upon his not understanding it!" —Upton Sinclair[250]

"If there is hope, it lies in the proles." —George Orwell, Nineteen Eighty-Four

---

[249] http://www.truth-out.org/news/item/25868-hawaiis-gmo-battle-federal-judge-strikes-down-kauais-pesticide-regulations and http://www.dailycamera.com/lafayette-news/ci_26417569/judge-tosses-out-lafayette-fracking-ban

[250] *I, Candidate for Governor: And How I Got Licked* (1935), ISBN 0-520-08198-6; University of California Press, 1994, p. 109.

Another necessary democratic restoration is local control over the police. Part of the cartel's objectives in creating the 9-11 event—in addition to their attempts to shred the Constitution, shut down public banks around the world,[251] steal natural resources, and secure geo-political advantage[252]—is the establishment of international control over military[253] and police units.[254]

A good example of the implementation of this is the manner in which the Occupy Wall Street movement was dismantled around the world. Here, in the U.S., the orders came from the FBI,[255] yet the same orders were also carried out globally. Another example is the NYPD slowdown (December, 2014—January, 2015) in which police spokespersons attempted to shift the blame from themselves, for brutality and racism, onto the protesters, for violence (actually seeded by cartel-paid *agent provocateurs* and saboteurs), and the mayor, for "lack of support." What's come to light over these shameless tactics is that much of the police's overzealous day-to-day enforcement work is simply to compensate for deficiencies in tax collections,[256] because their masters have choked the money supply; in other words, the police are used to further pillage the populace. Any persons or public officials that oppose the police face their wrath.[257] The only difference between such behavior and that of the jack-booted, goose-stepping Nazi

---

[251] http://www.activistpost.com/2012/09/state-owned-central-banks-are-real.html

[252] http://screencast.com/t/10zrbuw9HQ

[253] http://truth-out.org/opinion/item/22784-chris-hedges-fighting-the-militarized-state

[254] http://www.dailykos.com/story/2014/08/19/1322763/-Using-the-ballot-box-to-lawfully-disarm-the-American-militarized-police-state-Police-execution-video

[255] http://www.theguardian.com/commentisfree/2012/dec/29/fbi-coordinated-crackdown-occupy and https://cryptome.org/2016/08/deep-politics-rev4.pdf

[256] http://readersupportednews.org/opinion2/277-75/27811-the-nypds-work-stoppage-is-surreal

[257] https://www.dailykos.com/story/2015/01/27/1360537/-Indisputable-proof-that-prosecutors-and-politicians-are-penalized-when-they-hold-police-accountable and https://boingboing.net/2015/11/08/police-union-threatens-surpr.html

brigades and Gestapo is a matter of degree: mostly a better public relations department—the corporate owned mass and social media.

Given the growing lawlessness of local police—murdering unarmed citizens, sexual assaults, etc.—it's time that their operations were returned to local civilian control and monitoring, including the mandatory use of video cameras on all personnel (and severe penalties for the failure to have the cameras operating, including dismissal and prosecution), monitored by independent community boards.[258]

While the power of the cartel appears more monolithic than any previously recorded earthly empire, it is important to remember that we are actually talking about a very small group of top controllers— approximately .000001% of the world's population. This is the reason that the cartel is so obsessed with lock-step obedience from its military and police troops, along with the cultivation of advanced weaponry and surveillance, including drones and robotic troops,[259] as well as with constant war: this is the only way for such a small group of people to maintain control over the world. When the police and military wake up to their use as cannon fodder for the cartel, all bets are off,[260] and democracy will, once again, be possible.

---

[258] http://www.truth-out.org/news/item/23463-wisconsin-passes-first-state-law-requiring-independent-investigations-of-police-custody-deaths

[259] https://www.technologyreview.com/s/601598/magic-leaps-latest-surprise-its-working-on-robots If they are going public with this, it has already advanced much further in top-secret military and intelligence programs.

[260] http://www.huffingtonpost.com/2013/06/20/police-join-protesters-brazil_n_3474354.html, http://www.theneonnettle.com/videos/486-police-worldwide-start-laying-down-weapons-in-support-for-the-99-, http://countercurrentnews.com/2016/11/happening-cops-leave-standing-rock-refuse-return/#, http://miniplanet.us/veterans-deploy-to-standing-rock-to-engage-the-enemy-the-us-government/, http://www.mintpressnews.com/veterans-joining-forces-standing-rock-protestors-north-dakota/222513/, https://wearechange.org/police-thailand-join-protestors/,

https://www.democracynow.org/2017/12/4/honduras_protesters_defy_military_c rackdown_and, and https://www.theguardian.com/world/2017/dec/04/honduras- election-board-refrains-from-declaring-winner-as-violence-continues.
150

STEP 6—RESTORING LAW, SCIENCE, AND LOGIC

*"We are grateful to **The Washington Post, The New York Times, Time Magazine** and other great publications whose directors have attended our meetings and respected their promises of discretion for almost forty years. We would have found it quite impossible to develop our global project if we had been subject to the public spotlight during these years. But, the world has grown more sophisticated and willing to move towards a global government that no longer knows war, but only peace and prosperity for all of humanity. The supranational sovereignty of an intellectual elite and world bankers is surely preferable to the national self-determination practiced in past centuries." —David Rockefeller, June 5, 1991*[261]

The lords of misrule

Thus, forty-seven years after the Bretton Woods Conference set up Federal Reserve Notes to become the world reserve currency, David Rockefeller declared that the self-described "New World Order" (NWO) had sewn up control over the planet. Given the various illicit

---

[261] In an address to the Bilderberger meeting in Baden Baden, Germany (a meeting also attended by then-Governor Bill Clinton), as reported and translated from the September, 1991, issue of the Monte Carlo-based *Hilaire du Berrier Report* (also reported elsewhere in the French press, including *Minutes*, June 19, 1991 and *Lectures Francaises*, July/August, 1991). Mr. Du Berrier closely followed and chronicled the activities of Bilderberg and its overlapping groups, for over four decades.

means by which this plutocracy seized power, it is fitting that we revisit the premise of the Nuremberg Trials:

> "If certain acts and violations of treaties are crimes, they are crimes whether the United States does them or whether Germany does them. We are not prepared to lay down a rule of criminal conduct against others which we would not be willing to have invoked against us." —U.S. Supreme Court Justice Robert Jackson, the chief prosecutor of the Nuremberg War Crimes Trials following World War II

The crimes of the Rockefellers, the Rothschilds, and less than a dozen other families—that sit atop the pyramid of control[262] over almost all of the world's corporations (including the mass and social media and voting machines), governments (including military and intelligence operations), and natural resources—are numerous, including:

- Crimes against humanity[263]
- Treason[264]
- Murder
- Racketeering and fraud[265]
- Conspiracy

Given that no one from the .000001% has ever been tried for their crimes, we must consider how they came to control the legal system, before we can offer a strategy for the re-establishment of law, as well

[262] www.newscientist.com/article/mg21228354.500-revealed--the-capitalist-network-that-runs-the-world.html
[263] http://readersupportednews.org/opinion2/277-75/27383-focus-release-of-six-detainees-after-twelve-years-highlights-the-historic-evil-of-guantanamo
[264] http://www.youtube.com/watch?v=O1GCeuSr3Mk
[265] http://www.nytimes.com/2014/12/07/us/politics/energy-firms-in-secretive-alliance-with-attorneys-general.html

as a scientific method governed by the power of reasoning, not by the exigencies of capital.

Ask not for whom the gavel tolls; it tolls for thee

In the U.S.A., a common assumption regarding the operations of its legal system is that the courts represent an independent branch of a sovereign government. However, as we have detailed, our government, including the red and blue parties, is nothing more than a public-sector subsidiary of the international banking cartel and its corporations.

Along the same historical timeline and by similar insidious means through which the cartel gained political power—that is, via privately owned central banks and currencies, in Great Britain, Europe, and the U.S.—we find that they also gained legal power and control over what is held up as rational thought, particularly what is passed off as law and science.

How the banking crime syndicate went legit

A lot has been written on this subject, much of it speculative, involving the fealty of attorneys and counsellors worldwide to the City of London, an independent financial district in the heart of Great Britain's capital city. Nevertheless, the lack of documentation for these arguments does not mean that the international banking cartel has not gained control over most of the world's legal systems; rather, observing the process from a different point-of-view, we find that there are many means by which cartel has gained control over legal systems, including:

- Diverting the law from protecting citizen's rights (labor) to protecting corporate rights (capital); that is, turning the criminal code into a commercial code for the benefit of the criminals who run it;

- Enabling court procedures and privileges for attorneys and denying them to others;[266]
- Enforcing their version of the law through assassinations, economic sabotage, famine, war, election theft, bribery, racketeering, internationalization of the military and police, etc.; and,
- Obfuscating the law, through complexity, legerdemain, and illogical judgments.

Let's look at the entities involved in the struggle for "legal" control of this country:

- The United States of America (U.S.A.): A confederation of sovereign states that grants certain rights to a federal government, which (only theoretically, at this time) serves at the pleasure of and in the interests of these states.
- Statutory code: The revised statutes of the individual and severable United States of America, for example, the Colorado Revised Statutes (CRS).
- The United States (U.S.): The federal government, originally created by representatives presuming to act in the interests of the United States of America.
- U.S. Code: United States Code (USC), i.e., the laws of the federal government.

The interplay between the legal codes for United States of America (U.S.A.) and the United States (U.S.), along with the actions of the

---

[266] For example, a letter of Feb. 5, 2015, from U.S. Department of Justice, Civil Rights Division, to Mr. Malik Basurto (regarding the ruling on his claim of racial discrimination), states that because he represented himself, he waived his right to due process. Further, it states that his decision to go *pro per* results in his "loss of rights to investigators, law libraries, the hiring of experts and other resources that is (*sic*) available to a civil attorney." Special privileges that go with "titles of nobility" (e.g., "Esquire") are forbidden by the Constitution, and the original (and suppressed) 13th Amendment, which we will discuss shortly.

international banking cartel, are one of the key dialectics to the history of this country, beginning in colonial times and continuing to the present.

The Constitution as a Coup d'État

When the Constitution of the United States of America was adopted in 1788, without the unanimous consent required by the Articles of Confederation, it ceded certain powers, previously exclusive to the states, to the federal government, with all other rights, expressed and unexpressed, remaining exclusive to the states; and yet, the cartel has seen to it that these powers of the federal government (the U.S.) have been expanded to give it increasing control over the states (the U.S.A.). Here's how they did it.

In the Articles of Confederation, enacted in 1781, the Congress ("the United States in Congress assembled") drafted "a plan of confederacy for securing the freedom, sovereignty, and independence of the United States of America" (the states individually and severally); but with the Constitution of the United States, enacted in 1788, the Congress of the Confederation created a federal entity that benefited the cartel (by centralizing power, thus making it easier to control the U.S.A.).

Clearly, the Congress of the Confederation violated the law of the land (the Articles of Confederation) by enacting the Constitution simply by declaring it to be so, and not by the requirements prescribed by the Articles of Confederation.[267] The operational result was a usurpation of

---

[267] Although the Articles of Confederation were eventually adopted by all the states, the period between the enactment of the Constitution and its actual passage was not only illegal, but was also, metaphorically speaking, "fruit of the poisonous tree," which allowed the Anglo-Euro-American banking cartel to purchase control of the ratification process in each of the remaining states.

the rights of the U.S.A. by the cartel.[268] In the big picture, this was just another criminal act in a long series of criminal acts, though nevertheless a key one, both in terms of the cartel's perceived power and its illusory nature, since everything that follows is "fruit of the poisonous tree."[269]

Ironically, even if one accepts the Constitution as valid, then the issue of the missing 13th Amendment provides grounds for nullifying all laws passed by the Congress after the point at which it was ratified by Virginia, March 12, 1819, which fulfilled the Constitutional requirement of ratification of Amendments by three-quarters of the states. The original, and still valid, 13th Amendment, which reiterates a section of Article I, Section 9, of the Constitution, prohibits any members of Congress from accepting a title of nobility, such as Esquire, used by attorneys, because it is bestowed by and demands fealty to a foreign power, in this case the bankers who control Great Britain via the International Bar Association. Thus, the Amendments and laws passed after this date are invalid, though they are enforced by

---

[268] "The legislatures, unfortunately, mostly appointed their delegates [Founding Fathers] from among their local wealthy elite. The delegates then ensconced themselves in secret session and proceeded to betray the charter under which they had been assembled. They discarded the Articles, and began debating and drafting a wholly new document, one that transferred sovereignty to a relatively strong central government. The delegates reneged on the States that had sent them, and took it upon themselves to speak directly for "We the People." Thus begins the preamble to their Constitution. In effect they accomplished a *coup d'etat*. They managed to design a system that would enable existing elites to continue to run the affairs of the new nation, as they had before, under the Crown, via a Constitution that for all the world seems to embody sound democratic principles. The system was consciously designed to facilitate elite rule and that is how it has functioned ever since." —Richard K. Moore, *Escaping the Matrix - Global Transformation: Why we need it and how we can get it*, The Cyberjournal Project, December 16, 2005.

[269] We use this legal term metaphorically to imply that all actions resulting from an unconstitutional initial action are unconstitutional.

an illegitimate government. Instead, after suppressing this Amendment, the cartel replaced it with one that attempts to destroy states' rights.[270]

Once the federal government (U.S.) was so vested, the "invisible hand" of the cartel got down to the business of increasing its power via control over national money creation, military and intelligence operations, the legislative, executive, and judicial branches,[271] as well as through assassinations, economic sabotage, famine, war, election theft, bribery, and racketeering.

Despite their overriding power and cutthroat tactics, the cartel continued to meet resistance from a handful of Presidents and Congressmen—as we saw in the previous chapter—the prime examples being the push back against privately owned central banks from the likes of Madison, Jackson, Taylor, and Lincoln. Nevertheless, the debt burden of the states continued to grow, through a cartel organized push for ill-conceived public works projects (also mentioned in the previous chapter), as well as the cartel's next war, that between the states.

As mentioned, the Civil War was the culmination of an attempt by the Anglo-Euro-American banking cartel to sever the unity of the states, drive the Union and the Confederacy into debt, and prevent the United States of America from issuing its own currency, which, eventually, would have put an end to the cartel's criminal conspiracy.

Forcing the U.S. to issue bonds in exchange for currency

---

[270] http://themillenniumreport.com/2015/10/the-missing-13th-amendment-no-lawyersallowed-in-public-office/#more-18986

[271] http://www.opednews.com/articles/The-Courts-Like-the-Legis-by-Chris-Hedges-Corporatocracy_FISA_Supreme-Court_Supreme-Court-SCOTUS-150619-168.html

Also, as noted, it appears that the banking cartel thought that Lincoln would have no choice but to borrow capital at the diabolical interest rate of 24 to 36 percent; however, Lincoln and his advisers understood money and the Constitution better than the bankers anticipated, and chose to issue sovereign dollars (Greenbacks)—on which the nation did not pay principal or interest—to outfit and underwrite the Union Army.

In response, the bankers spent generously, bribing the Congress to pass the next big unconstitutional breakthroughs in their conquest of the U.S.A: the National Banking Acts of 1863 and 1864, giving the cartel control over the money supply, by requiring the federal government (the U.S.) to issue bonds, and pay principal and interest on those bonds, in order to receive private bank notes, which had, in the absence of any further issuance of Lincoln's Greenbacks (following his assassination), become, by default, the unofficial legal tender for all debts public and private.

Uncle Sam grants himself an enterprise zone

Seven years after the National Banking Acts, in 1871, the cartel, through its subordinate public sector legislators (the Congress), incorporated the District of Columbia, creating a faux governmental enterprise zone that they owned and operated through the "legal" entity of the U.S. Strategically, this enabled the cartel's North American toehold, the U.S. (i.e., the federal government), to control its own land, separate from the United States of America (the states united and severable). Here's how they did it.

The original District of Columbia, as prescribed in 1791—pursuant to Article I, Section 8, paragraph 17, of the United States Constitution— included Alexandria County, Virginia (a large swath of land on the west side of the Potomac. This county was later retroceded to Virginia in 1846. In 1870, the independent City of Alexandria seceded from Alexandria County. In 1920, the name Arlington County was adopted, after Arlington House, the home of General Robert E. Lee, which stands on the grounds of what is now Arlington National Cemetery.

In 1871, the Congress passed the District of Columbia Organic Act, which repealed the individual charters of the cities of Washington and Georgetown and established a new territorial government for the whole of the remaining District of Columbia. Though Congress repealed the territorial government in 1874, the legislation created a single on-going government for the federal district.

In 1873, President Grant appointed Alexander Robey Shepherd to the post of governor. Shepherd authorized large-scale municipal projects, which greatly modernized Washington, but in doing so bankrupted the city. Following this "fortuitous" event, in 1874, Congress replaced the District's quasi-elected territorial government with an appointed three-member Board of Commissioners. Direct rule by Congress would continue for nearly a century until the passage of the District of Columbia Home Rule Act in 1973.

Since then, Congress has allowed certain powers of government to be carried out by locally elected officials while maintaining the power to overturn local laws and exercising greater oversight of the city than exists for any U.S. state. Furthermore, the District's elected government exists at the pleasure of Congress and could theoretically be revoked at any time.

In other words, the U.S. (the federal government) owns and operates its own district (the District of Columbia). This is why it would be a foolish strategy, for the international banking cartel that controls the federal government, to make D.C. a state: because the federal government would then be only "renting space" from an independent state. In addition, such statehood would reduce D.C. to equal terms with the other states, putting at risk the illegal hierarchical legal structure that masks the cartel's criminal choke hold over the sovereign states.

Once ensconced in their own plutocratic domain, the international banking cartel then focused on their agenda for destroying any remaining sovereignty in the U.S.A. and elsewhere.

The requirements for maintaining the "sound money" myth

One of the mythologies with which the cartel has been so successful down through the centuries is that of sound money. The pitch goes something like this: "These green pieces of paper are backed by gold, which has always been the measure of value." As we noted in detail in *Step 1*, paper currencies have never been backed by gold on a one-to-one basis, but rather by the same leveraging method that originally enabled goldsmiths to take over the banking functions of the formerly sovereign states of Europe, i.e., holding only a portion of the private currency's face value in gold.

Nevertheless, it was a convenient myth, since it allowed the central bankers—who control and manipulate the markets for stocks, bonds, commodities (perishables and precious metals), and mortgages (MERS), as well as interest rates (LIBOR)[272]—to move value from one currency to another via gold, or to use gold as a store of value while they speculate and destroy currencies, as a run-up to stealing the natural resources and other assets from the nation-states of issue.

Given the limitations of the gold supply relative to the goods and services in circulation,[273] as well as the cumbersome nature of exchanging gold, the bankers needed to create a single national bank

---

[272] See our overview in *Step 3*, or a more detailed list at: http://coloradopublicbanking.blogspot.com/2015/02/the-running-tab-on-bank-fraud.html

[273] http://www.bloomberg.com/news/2014-12-11/commodities-trader-gunvor-said-to-exit-gold-trading-after-a-year.html

note that would serve as an alternative to gold, a precious metal which they would rather reserve as the last resort store-of-value for the value that they have stolen from labor.

One obstacle to this plan was the availability of silver ("free silver") across the general population, through mining claims and foundries (mints). Thus, as noted in the last chapter, in 1873, over strenuous protests that lasted decades, silver was demonetized, essentially making gold the monetary standard, thereby eliminating money creation outside of the cartel's purveyance.

At this point, in terms of legal status, in addition to the previously acquired and usurped powers from the states, we now have the U.S. (the federal government) paying principal and interest to spend and circulate, into the marketplace, various private bank notes owned and operated by the cartel, with the further ruse that this paper is backed by gold. This sleight-of-hand continued on, even after the creation of the Federal Reserve System (1913), eventually and magically conjuring the illusion that Fort Knox was filled will a sufficient supply of gold to back all the Federal Reserve Notes in circulation.[274]

Bankruptcy of the United States

From our present vantage point, we can see that bankruptcy strategies have been enforced for centuries on enemies of the cartel. (Recently, these strategies have expanded from nation-states to states and cities, such as Detroit.[275]) So, after 1913, with the cartel now in control of the central bank (the Federal Reserve System), which was selling private bank notes to the U.S.—and after the establishment of a federal income

---

[274] There is no legitimate audit, past or present, that vouches for the quantity and quality of these gold reserves.

[275] http://coloradopublicbanking.blogspot.com/2013/08/detroit-and-your-hometown-how-banks.html

tax and the Internal Revenue Service, to pay the interest for the use of the cartel's private paper—the focus for bankrupting the U.S.[276] shifted from the issuance of a single national private bank note (achieved) to maximizing the debt owed by the U.S., and its newly conjured taxpayers, to the cartel.

And what better way to achieve this than creating the First World War?

The vampire squid and its tendrils

Wars are, as noted, a tried and true tactic of the cartel for quickly driving up debt. Government "leaders" are either on board with this program, or they are deposed and disposed.

Following the First World War, the Roaring Twenties—fueled by low margins (20% for purchasing securities)—ran up private personal and commercial debt, all the while creating a surfeit of collateralized assets, which were later acquired for mills on the dollar, when the cartel crashed the system and imposed the Great Depression on the planet.[277]

During this severe contraction of the money supply, the U.S. (federal) government was in need of massive funds to rebuild the nation, while navigating between the cartel-manufactured twin terrors of fascism and "communism."[278] There was only one entity that possessed the license

---

[276] https://www.youtube.com/watch?v=I-Mpm_EALH8

[277] Both Milton Friedman and Ben Bernanke are on record as saying the Fed caused the Great Depression. http://www.wnd.com/2008/03/59405/

[278] In the run up to WWII, the Union Banking Corporation (the Bushes, the Harrimans, and the Dulles brothers) invested in and laundered money for Fritz Thyssen and the Nazi war machine, not to mention the outright support by the Rockefeller's Standard Oil (supplying oil) and Thomas Watson's IBM (keeping track of concentration camp prisoners) for the Nazis. It's also worth noting that the western bankers backed Lenin, in order to overthrow the provisional Russian

to print the requisite bank notes needed to pay for the New Deal, and that was the cartel, behind its pseudo-legal sanctification of the Fed as the central bank of the U.S., and Federal Reserve Notes as "legal tender."

Thus, FDR was at the helm of an insolvent public sector subsidiary corporation, otherwise known as the U.S. There could be no other explanation, since the U.S. was not sovereign, by virtue of: 1) losing the right to print its own money in 1863 and 1864, and 2) having its currency formally usurped in 1913. The U.S. was thereby forced into a form of national bankruptcy that was presented as the only viable solution, with the international banking cartel gaining effective receivership ("mortgagees in possession," as the ABA called it in 1913) over the federal government. Whether or not this was a formal and legal receivership is beside the point, since it was the culmination of various criminal actions down through the centuries ("fruit of the poisonous tree"); but, nevertheless, it was, operationally, a receivership.[279]

Beginning with the Emergency Banking Act, on March 9, 1933, which was followed by Executive Order 6102[280]—criminalizing the possession of monetary gold by any individual, partnership, association, or corporation, with Congress passing a similar resolution in June 1933—the cartel was given *carte blanche* to loan to the U.S.

---

government under Kerensky, which had established a state-owned central bank. Thus, fascism and so-called communism were both funded by the cartel.

[279] The other key factor being Roosevelt's willingness to go along with the cartel's plan. As noted by Carroll Quigley: "One of the most significant facts about the New Deal was Its orthodoxy on money. For the whole twelve years he was in the White House, Roosevelt had statutory power to issue fiat money in the form of greenbacks printed by the government without recourse to the banks. This authority was never used." (*Tragedy and Hope*, Volumes 1-8, The Macmillan Company, New York, 1966)

[280] In all, the related legislation included Executive Orders 6073, 6102, 6111, and 6260, House Joint Resolution 192 of June 5, 1933 confirmed in Perry v. U.S. (1935) 294 U.S. 330-381, 79 LEd 912, as well as 31 United States Code (USC) 5112, 5119 and 12 USC 95a.

whatever amount necessary to re-establish a banking system that guaranteed customers' bank deposits and put the nation's labor force back to work. In the process, all gold money (other than collectibles) was to be turned over to the U.S. Thus, the faux currency of the U.S. (Federal Reserve Notes) took another step in detaching itself from gold, even as the cartel was stealing the gold it collected in the name of economic necessity. How could this be? Because monetized gold was, by edict, removed from the marketplace.

As a result of these "laws," a permanent debt relationship was established between the "too big to fail" (TBTF) banks that own the Federal Reserve—by virtue of their capitalization[281] and control over the voting members of each Federal Reserve District (see report of the 1976 House of Representatives Committee on Banking[282])—and the legal entity of the U.S. (the federal government).

Where did all of the collected gold go?

Given the various intrigues regarding gold deposits, including the famous story of tungsten bars coated with gold,[283] and the eventual (2004) bowing out of the City of London firm of NW Rothschild from setting the price of gold, the question of the destination of the gold collected by Roosevelt's dictum is a compelling mystery. But as noted previously, there is never enough gold to back a currency, because the production of gold never equals the increase in goods and services being traded in the marketplace. That is why, in instances when gold is declared the only currency (such as when Parliament banned paper currencies in the American colonies), depressions necessarily follow.

---

[281] http://www.opednews.com/articles/Call-me-crazy-but-I-like-by-Henry-Porter-101202-267.html

[282] http://www.scribd.com/doc/46627723/Federal-Reserve-Directors-A-Study-of-Corporate-and-Banking-Influence-Staff-Report-Committee-on-Banking-Currency-and-Housing-House-of-Representative

[283] http://www.cnbc.com/id/43391588#

Yet, the ruse continued. In 1944, the Bretton Woods Conference (the United Nations Monetary and Financial Conference) obligated each country to adopt a monetary policy that maintained the exchange rate, by tying its currency to gold, and made the IMF a backstop to bridge temporary imbalances of payments.

Then came the back end of the double switch—the final blow to the smoke and mirrors of "sound money"—when the cartel, acting through its proxy, Great Britain, asked the U.S. to redeem $3 billion in Federal Reserve Notes for gold (at $35 per ounce), "forcing" Nixon to detach FRNs from gold on August 15, 1971.

Essentially, the cartel was now admitting that Federal Reserve Notes (FRNs) were a free-floating (*private*) fiat currency. Nevertheless, the result was to formally transfer the function of the lowest common denominator of value (the world reserve currency) from gold to FRNs. In simple terms, this meant that the cartel owned the printing press for the currency with which they could buy, and thus control, the world.

And what happened to all the gold that was collected? As noted earlier, gold is a useful hedge when currencies need to be attacked, to enable the theft of resources from the target nation-state of the moment. But this is just one aspect of gold's role in achieving world domination.

All the gold that was collected, along with gold previously held, found its way to a secret account within the Treasury Department, called the Exchange Stabilization Fund (ESF) that, on the surface, was instituted to protect FRNs on the world currency exchanges. But in practice, the ESF became the slush fund for all U.S. intelligence related black ops throughout the world,[284] as well as the key lever for propping up Federal Reserve Notes.[285] Thus, the value of the gold that the cartel

---

[284] http://www.zerohedge.com/news/presenting-exchange-stabilization-fund-5-parts-real-plunge-protection-team

[285] https://www.youtube.com/watch?v=2ssrcD5GdPQ

now controlled, untethered from the currency, would grow significantly in value, giving its intelligence and military operations a significant hidden endowment, that would later be supplemented with vast sums supposedly lost, or at least untracked via accounting legerdemain, by the Pentagon.[286]

What rule of law?

> "Permit me to issue and control the money of a nation, and I care not who makes its laws!" —Apocryphal quote attributed to Meyer Amschel Rothschild

So, we see that by hijacking the legal framework of the U.S.A. (the sovereign states, united and severable) via a federal government, the cartel was able to privatize U.S. currency and leverage its private bank notes (FRNs) to buy up whatever other resources (natural and human) necessary to attain suzerainty over the U.S.A. and much of the world.

Undermining States' Rights

Due to the original sovereign standing of the states, united but severable, the next strategic step was for the cartel to alter state constitutions and city charters to ensure that all credit be licensed to private banks, rather than sovereign bodies politic and corporate.

Thus began the insertion of specific prohibitions into various existent and newly created state constitutions and city charters that prohibited these previously sovereign entities from creating banks that leveraged taxpayer dollars in the public interest; so, just as the Articles of Confederation were hijacked by the cartel's Constitution, a Federalist Trojan horse, so did the states and their legal frameworks fall victim to the cartel's statutory poison pill templates, much as the American

---

[286] https://www.youtube.com/watch?v=xU4GdHLUHwU

Legislative Exchange Council (ALEC), and its derivative organizations and disguises, continue to decimate the rights of the people today.

For example, in the Colorado Constitution—as interpreted by the legislative, executive, and judicial branches of the Colorado state government—the state has no right to create a publicly owned bank that would "lend or pledge" the state's credit. What this means exactly is open to interpretation, which is how the cartel likes it, because if you control the players, legal gobbledygook gives your minions the leeway to make up the law as they go along, as we noted in *Step 5*, regarding our efforts to get the question of a publicly owned state bank on the Colorado ballot through the initiative process. Ironically, a state bank would do exactly the opposite of pledging the state's credit: it would be facilitating loans where others pledge their credit, just like the Bank of North Dakota has done successfully for over 99 years.[287] Regardless, officials in Colorado pretend not to understand this, because they are paid to act in the cartel's interest, not that of the electorate, whom they pretend to represent.

Fascism and "the People's Republic of Boulder"

The same holds true at the county and city level—jurisdictions that have fallen like dominoes to the cartel's American version of fascism (corporate control over the state)—even those entities that see themselves as progressive; for example, in the City of Boulder, Colorado and Boulder County, Colorado, we see how pressure exerted by the cartel prevents progressive evolutionary development.

After the citizens of the City of Boulder twice defeated Xcel Energy at the ballot box in their drive to create a city-owned public utility that would accelerate the timeline for the use of renewable energy to power

---

[287] http://coloradopublicbanking.blogspot.com/2013/05/how-nations-states-counties-and-cities.html

the local grid, the banking empire struck back using their now government-admitted HAARP weapon[288] to bring a "1,000-year flood"—a stationary weather pattern drawing upon moist gulf air to destroy the canyons, cities, and plains of Boulder County—to drive up the debt of the locals to the cartel. It should also be noted that the second electoral defeat of Xcel Energy came with a price,[289] an Xcel sponsored debt limitation initiative designed to hamstring the city's efforts. So far, the City of Boulder, fully backed by two successful votes, has spent approximately $10 million to get Xcel to accede to the voters' demands. Recently, the city turned down Xcel's "settlement" offer,[290] while Xcel management claims they are not obstructing the process.[291]

One would hope that such an anomalistic event as a 10-day "rainstorm" in the arid west would raise local consciousness regarding the technological power of the cartel, as well as the seriousness with which they defend their choke hold over most of the planet. Unfortunately, Boulder's radicalism has, since the '60's, generally confined itself to environmental issues, not political and economic ones. Of course, there are many who cannot conceive of "the U.S. government" doing anything to its allies and citizens, but this is a misconception of the nature of the power structure. To the cartel, any take-back of assets (banking, energy, healthcare, education, etc.) by the public is seen as

---

[288] http://themindunleashed.org/2014/05/conspiracy-theorists-vindicated-haarp-confirmed-weather-manipulation-tool.html and
http://www.globalresearch.ca/the-ultimate-weapon-of-mass-destruction-owning-the-weather-for-military-use-2/5306386 It's worth noting that a company in Russia has developed a similar weapon, which means their government has a more sophisticated version: http://tass.com/science/960090
[289] http://www.dailycamera.com/boulder-election-news/ci_24459325/boulder-ballot-issue-310-2e-municipalization
[290] http://www.bizjournals.com/denver/news/2017/04/18/boulder-council-votes-to-move-forward-on-city.html
[291] http://www.dailycamera.com/news/boulder/ci_31189652/xcel-denies-obstructing-boulder-bid-energy-independence

an enemy act. To maintain the charade of nation-states and old enmities, "invisible" weapons are used on "friendly" nations, states, and cities—and one variety of those weapons create climatic and geologic events. Japan, New Zealand, and others have felt this wrath, for daring to maintain their public banks.[292]

The City of Boulder and Boulder County are in a perfect situation to leverage public banking to underwrite the build-out of a publicly owned utility, a strategy that would allow the work to be completed at half the cost; yet, neither the CFO of the City nor the Treasurer of the County, based upon our conversations with them, were willing, in the case of the former, or able, in the case of the latter, to consider such an option. City councilpersons offer the same tired excuses as well.[293] In addition, the City of Boulder has let the cartel's disruption of its tax base (from the 2008 money supply contraction) create a dependency on corporate programs that prey upon citizens; for example, allowing corporate automobile traffic monitoring systems to be set with short yellow light durations to drive up ticket revenues and increase accident probability. While Boulder still has a much better tax base than Detroit, it is no less a public-sector subsidiary of the cartel. Another example of this subservience is the county's use of JPMorgan Chase credit cards to distribute heat and food subsidies for the poor. Why should the cartel profit from these social programs paid for by taxpayers?

> "Since I entered politics, I have chiefly had men's views confided to me privately. Some of the biggest men in the United States, in the field of commerce and manufacture, are afraid of somebody, are afraid of something. They know that there is a power somewhere so organized, so subtle, so watchful, so interlocked, so complete, so pervasive, that they had better not

---

[292] http://www.geoengineeringwatch.org/massive-us-senate-document-on-national-and-global-weather-modification/

[293] http://www.dailycamera.com/columnists/ci_31529474/jan-burton-first-city-owned-utility-next-city

speak above their breath when they speak in condemnation of it." —Woodrow Wilson, *The New Freedom: A Call For the Emancipation of the Generous Energies of a People*, Section I: "The Old Order Changeth," p. 13

"If ye love wealth greater than liberty, the tranquility of servitude greater than the animating contest for freedom, go home from us in peace. We seek not your counsel nor your arms. Crouch down and lick the hand that feeds you. May your chains set lightly upon you; and may posterity forget that ye were our countrymen." —Samuel Adams

"Of course we will have fascism in America, but we will call it democracy!" —Huey Long

But the subversion of law and representative government is only one area in which the destruction of reasoning and language enables the destruction of freedom.

Science in Advanced Fascist Societies

Using the term "science" or "scientific" these days tends to draw allegiance from those who believe that such terminology somehow guarantees a reasoned approach to the data at hand; but, as history has shown, scientific standards are, each in their own time, often not much different than religious dogma, in the sense that what is insisted upon turns out to be inaccurate or wrong[294]; worse, science is often subordinated to the objectives of those who own and control the state; for example, in Nazi Germany, Einstein's theories were derided as "Jewish science."[295] In the U.S., the banks and their corporations and

---

[294] http://www.nytimes.com/2015/08/28/science/many-social-science-findings-not-as-strong-as-claimed-study-says.html and
http://reason.com/archives/2016/08/26/most-scientific-results-are-wrong-or-use
[295] www.nytimes.com/2012/08/05/books/review/einsteins-jewish-science-by-steven-gimbel.html

public sector subsidiaries (federal and state governments) control grant moneys for research, so those not willing to go along with the sponsored groupthink are often left without funding and publicity.[296]

Take the issue of climate change. Those who believe that it is a scientific fact that the burning of fossil fuels alone (or in combination with methane releases as tundra is exposed) is causing global warming, and who ridicule anyone who believes otherwise, are missing a few key facts that belie any pretense for their "scientific method."

The known data includes: the burning of fossil fuels and the attendant smog, measurements such as average temperatures in various locales, the melting of the ice shelfs, as well as extreme weather, including severe droughts, floods, earthquakes, tsunamis, etc.

Those subscribing to "global warming" express the aforementioned data as: the burning of fossil fuels = global warming and extreme weather. This line of reasoning, if it can be called that, leaves out major factors, including the capability of military and intelligence programs to create and use weather and geologic events as weapons.[297] Of course, the standard "scientific" response to this is to fall back on the common logical fallacies of *ad hominem* or *appeal to emotions*, using it in the form of calling their detractors "conspiracy theorists." But now that government scientists have admitted to what they call geo-engineering—not to mention that, in the late 1990's: 1) the EU Parliament asked the U.S. to come clean on its HAARP program; 2) the Canadian Broadcasting System did a documentary on HAARP; and 3) the U.S. Air Force published a tract on owning the weather by

---

[296] http://www.intellectualtakeout.org/blog/most-scientific-studies-today-are-fake-science

[297] http://themindunleashed.org/2014/05/conspiracy-theorists-vindicated-haarp-confirmed-weather-manipulation-tool.html and
http://www.geoengineeringwatch.org/massive-us-senate-document-on-national-and-global-weather-modification/

2025[298]—such logical fallacies hold no water. If there is any conspiracy here, it is that of so-called scientists promulgating ignorance of the political, economic, and military/intelligence forces to which we are subject.

Similarly, campaigns and elections involving the so-called "two party system" ignore the influence of the cartel and its long reach through cross ownership and interlocking directorates—including over the media, polling organizations, and voting machines—when discussing the published vote totals. Elections where electronic voting and counting machines tabulate are not verifiable. In fact, it has been shown over and over[299] that the hacking of electronic voting machines (from domestic sources, not Russia[300]) is the norm,[301] not the aberration.

So much for "science" as it is practiced by those whose understanding of the power structure never ventures outside the box of what has been fed them from the corporate-owned media and educational institutions, or by those who are paid to obfuscate the truth.

What is "scientific method" or empiricism?

Scientific method is nothing more than a means to ask and answer questions by making observations and doing experiments. In general, the steps of scientific method are:

- Ask a question

---

[298] http://csat.au.af.mil/2025/volume3/vol3ch15.pdf

[299] http://codered2014.com/

[300] https://www.activistpost.com/2017/11/wikileaks-vault-8-part-1-cia-wrote-code-impersonate-anti-virus-company-kaspersky-lab.html and http://coloradopublicbanking.blogspot.com/2017/01/us-intelligence-reports-fail.html

[301] http://declarationofaccountability.com/problems-and-solutions/electoral-accountability

- Do background research
- Construct a hypothesis, including a control group
- Test your hypothesis by doing an experiment
- Analyze your data and draw a conclusion
- Communicate your results[302]
- Update your hypothesis as data reveals new actions/behaviors

In other words, scientific method is, at its best, an operational truth that works until it doesn't. One of the most common flaws in scientific methodology is to ignore having a control group, or to choose a control group that is missing key factors, as in our example above regarding climate change.

Therefore, when you read that a climate model "proves" global warming, you know immediately that such a statement is non-scientific. A model or a hypothesis cannot "prove" anything, only venture to show a process that produces the known data. But new data can always invalidate a hypothesis or model, just as Einstein described the "key" to empiricism when he said:

> "The case is never closed." And,

> "Many experiments may prove me right but it takes only one to prove me wrong."[303]

The politics of science and the science of politics

The means of funding contemporary scientific research is, principally, the federal government, with additional hefty supplements from large foundations and corporations. All of these sources have specific political agendas based on their owners and controllers, who are,

---

[302] http://www.sciencebuddies.org/science-fair-projects/project_scientific_method.shtml

[303] http://climateclash.com/2-the-scientific-method/

generally speaking, the same set of persons subject to the same groupthink. As we noted in *Step 3*, their objectives are, simply stated: power, profit, propaganda, and population reduction.

As a result, contemporary science serves the objectives of a very small minority[304] (.000001%), and not the objectives of the people (99.999999%) and the evolution of human consciousness and its application in the public interest; i.e., "... life, liberty, and the pursuit of happiness." As noted earlier, and which bears repeating here:

> "In the face of the totalitarian features of this society, the traditional notion of the "neutrality" of technology can no longer be maintained. Technology as such cannot be isolated from the use to which it is put; the technological "society" is a system of domination which operates already in the concept and construction of techniques." —Herbert Marcuse, *One-Dimensional Man*, 1964

The bottom line

In a fascist society, information and technology derived from scientific research is *always* vetted first for military and intelligence applications, to ensure that a very small number of beings are able to maintain their hegemony over the human race. When such information and technology is released to the public, usually decades after its discovery and development, any public use will be limited in some manner; for example, enabling intelligence organizations access to all Internet[305]

---

[304] https://jonrappoport.wordpress.com/2015/08/25/to-science-bloggers-living-with-mommy/ and https://ethicalnag.org/2009/11/09/nejm-editor/
[305] http://mashable.com/2013/07/31/nsa-xkeyscore/

and cell phone activity[306] via various backdoors embedded by the intelligence agencies themselves.[307]

As we have seen throughout this book, the root cause of global dysfunction at every level is private control over money creation and the leveraging of this into legal, political, economic, military, and scientific control. While this consolidation of power may seem insurmountable, history shows, if nothing else, that such immutable judgments are never accurate.

So, what tools do we have to address the restoration of law and scientific method?

Education and legal recourse

Given the power of the banking cartel and the present allegiance of the military and police to this criminal conspiracy, the first objective in changing the present dystopia—before we can invoke Justice Jackson's prescription quoted at the beginning of this chapter—must be in educating large numbers of people.

In terms of the law, there are a few tactics that, if employed by the people locally across the nation, could serve to educate the unaware as to the current power structure and the objectives of those at the top. These include:

---

[306] http://www.theguardian.com/world/2013/dec/04/nsa-storing-cell-phone-records-daily-snowden and
http://www.news10.net/story/news/investigations/watchdog/2014/03/06/cellphone-spying-technology-used-throughout-northern-california/6144949/
[307] http://www.mintpressnews.com/wikileaks-cia-bugging-factory-fresh-iphones-since-2008/226201/

Common law grand juries[308]: Although these citizen initiatives have come to be associated with reactionary organizations that combine anti-government sentiments and bigotry, the framework of these bodies is such that they can be used by progressives to seek remedy from the misuse of our government through criminal usurpation.

For example: "Given the repetitive premeditated frauds of the financial services industry (which we enumerated in *Step 3*), it would make sense to charge the executives of the "too-big-to-fail" banks with racketeering;" or, "Given the amoral, psychopathic, and sociopathic behavior of banking executives,[309] petitions regarding the criminally insane would also be in order."

An ambitious common law grand jury could even seek an indictment of any "elected" or appointed official who enforces laws that are "fruit of the poisonous tree," meaning a prosecution based on any laws these "officials" enacted to usurp the Bill of Rights for individuals, and the consequent justification of the assignment of these rights to corporations. Such laws are, according to the Constitution, illegal and therefore void. Part of the common law grand jury's reasoning would be that the courts have upheld the Preamble to the United States Constitution as evidence of the fundamental purposes, guiding principles, and intentions of the social contract. The contract includes "... the general Welfare ... the Blessings of Liberty to ourselves and our Posterity." It follows that any laws or series of laws enabled by unconstitutional actions—which obstruct, circumvent, or suppress

---

[308] http://www.fl-counties.com/docs/default-source/legal-documents-links/common-law-citizens-grand-jury-rules.pdf

309

http://www.alternet.org/story/152639/study%3A_wealthy_stockbrokers_more_dangerous_than_psychopaths

these purposes—are void,[310] and those seeking to enforce them are in violation of the law.

In addition, citizens in a few states have found a way to *circumvent prosecutors* and police who are beholden to the money masters,[311] via another generally unknown power: that of *jury annulment*[312] of laws, which allows any jury to judge an accused as "not culprit," even if the jury knows that the accused is guilty according the law as it is written. For example: "Given the unjust manner in which the banks and their corporations have usurped the sovereignty of the people of the United States of America, almost any law enacted and used against the people and not applied to the elite and their corporations, including the Internal Revenue Code, could be seen to be unjust, or even unconstitutional, and therefore annulled by a jury in determining its verdict."

An additional strategy is the formation of the "National General Assembly of the United States" (NGAOTUS). Here's the idea:

- Article V of the US Constitution provides a few different means for passing amendments. In addition to ¾ of the state legislatures passing an amendment, there is a provision for "conventions" in ¾ of the states. There is no specification for who can hold these conventions.
- NGAOTUS would attempt to be incorporated under 5 USC 104 as an Independent Establishment of the United States of America, *not* the U.S. corporation incorporated by the cartel.

---

[310] By the same token, the people could prosecute the federal government via a common law grand jury, nullify their tax payments under a common law set-off, given the approximately $21 trillion, all of which remains unaccounted by the Pentagon; for example, https://www.youtube.com/watch?v=67mkesJLWIY

[311] http://www.nytimes.com/2015/06/09/us/cleveland-leaders-bypass-prosecutors-to-seek-charge-in-tamir-rice-case.html

[312] http://lawyers-help.org/what-is-the-annulment-of-the-jury/

- NGAOTUS would then organize conventions in the 50 states. Each of the conventions would vote on the same amendment, which would include all the necessary stipulations to change the banking and monetary systems, hold verifiable elections, and decentralize the media.
- If these amendments pass ¾ of the conventions, we would have enforceable Constitutional stipulations that would override U.S. Code (which, in fact, is not a criminal code; rather, it is a code written by criminals).

Finally, one power that is beginning to get traction is the strong legal case of the U.S. Constitutional guarantee of state and local powers superseding federal powers, including that of county sheriffs as the highest law enforcement officer within their jurisdiction.[313] While this movement originated with conservative organizations, we hope that progressives, i.e., those outside the manufactured political consensus of the red and blue parties, will take note that the federal government has recognized its own limits as well as the power of county sheriffs within their jurisdiction. Even if we find other rulings by the Supreme Court to be reprehensible, it would be foolish for us to ignore the opportunity and fortuitous opinion expressed, in the case of Mack/Printz v. USA (in which portions of the Brady bill were declared unconstitutional), by Antonin Scalia and the majority:

Writing for the majority, the *late* Justice Scalia opined,[314] "... the Constitution's conferral upon Congress of not all governmental powers, but only discreet, enumerated ones."

Also, citing the Tenth Amendment, which affirms the limited powers doctrine, Scalia wrote that:

"The powers not delegated to the United States by the

---

[313] http://constitutionallawenforcementassoc.blogspot.com/

[314] http://constitutionallawenforcementassoc.blogspot.com/

Constitution ... are reserved to the States respectively, or to the people."

"It is incontestable that the Constitution established a system of dual sovereignty" and that the states retained "a residuary and inviolable sovereignty."

He goes further and cites James Madison, considered to be the father of our Constitution:

"The local or municipal authorities form distinct and independent portions of the supremacy, no more subject, within their respective spheres, to the general authority [federal government] than the general authority is subject to them, within its own sphere." (*The Federalist #39*)

The *majority* opinion goes on to say that "This separation of the two spheres is one of the constitution's structural protections of liberty. Just as the separation and independence of the coordinate branches of the federal government serve to prevent the accumulation of excessive power in any one branch, a healthy balance of power between the States and the Federal Government will reduce the risk of tyranny and abuse from either front."

Scalia again quotes Madison,[315] who says:

"Hence, a double security arises to the rights of the people. The different governments will control each other, at the same time that each will be controlled by itself." (*The Federalist #51*)

---

[315] Remember that President James Madison refused to renew the charter of the First Bank of the United States—which was Alexander Hamilton's sellout of the fledgling nation to the very forces who controlled Britain and the Bank of England, and who had hired mercenaries to fight the colonists—thus precipitating the War of 1812, from which the banking cartel, via its subsidiary, the British government, sought to re-take control over its former colonies' monetary system.

Essentially, this means that the state and county governments are actually and literally charged with controlling the federal government. To do so is, as emphasized above, "one of the Constitution's structural protections of liberty."

Clearly, the office of county sheriff, by law and in practice, holds supreme authority within its jurisdiction and can be used to shield local sovereignty against the cartel and its racketeers, which, in Colorado alone, have attempted to preempt local laws on such issues as minimum wage, rent control, community broadband, cyanide heap leach mining, high-volume hydraulic fracturing ("fracking"), plastic bag bans, gun safety laws, and factory farming. The cartel's proxies (led by the Colorado Bankers Association) ability to do so rests on a series of laws that have gutted the initiative process in Colorado, in violation of the state's constitution and preamble, which clearly states that the citizens of the states are the highest authority and that they can change the social contract when it so suits them.

Escape from manufactured consensus

For these tools to be effective, however, requires that sufficient numbers of people understand:

- The root cause of global dysfunction is private control over money creation;
- The cartel—through ownership of the media, polling organizations, and electronic voting machines, in addition to the educational process—aims to make citizens feel that they are part of a powerless minority; and
- The necessity of each person taking responsibility for his or her own spiritual evolution—which we examine in the next chapter, the seventh and final step required for global transformation.

Step 7—Taking humanity's next evolutionary step

"We must love one another or die." –W. H. Auden, from his poem "September 1, 1939"

Before we focus on *Step 7*, let's recap the key points in the first six steps, so that we may see more clearly the logical progression that connects economic and spiritual transformation. Our confidence in being able to show the natural connection between the marketplace and our higher consciousness stems from the implications of Solomon's Proof,[316] which explains how science and spirituality converge in the event of Singularity, i.e., a state of total unity.

In many ways, Singularity is the most generic and abstract concept in both science and spirituality. In scientific terms, Singularity is, by definition, the first dimension (space), in which everything that ever was, is, or will be is present now (time), because the entire potential of the universe is contained in Singularity; in spiritual terms, the most generic form of Deity is comprised of omniscience, omnipresence, and omnipotence. As you can see, these two sets of descriptions—for Singularity and Deity—are essentially identical to each other. Einstein discussed his insights on this in a letter to his daughter.[317]

The convergence of science and spirituality

On a more concrete level, the convergence of the social science of economics with a non-dogmatic spiritual practice is best illustrated, as

---

[316] http://www.solomonsproof.com
[317] https://wearelightbeings.wordpress.com/2015/04/15/a-letter-from-albert-einstein-to-his-daughter-about-the-universal-force-which-is-love/

we've discussed, by the story of Jesus using a whip to drive the money lenders out of the temple, and calling them "Thieves!" These actions indicate that Jesus, or the author of this story, clearly understood that usury is a crime against humanity. If you don't believe it, let's once again consider the oldest known testament, which escaped the editing process to which the *New Testament* was subject. In that scroll, it says:

> "If you have money, do not lend it at interest, but give it to one from whom you will not get it back." —*The Gospel of Thomas* (95).[318]

The effects of usury have been well known for millennia. There was a time when Jubilee years were declared by monarchs and tribal leaders, to remove all indebtedness and slavery created by interest and private control over money creation. By 33 C.E., when Jesus cleansed the Temple, every member of the Roman Senate was a usurer.[319] No wonder he was crucified shortly after this protest. The many inspired classical paintings of that act are the true symbols of his teachings— not the cross.

---

[318] *The Gospel of Thomas* and other texts found at Nag Hammadi (*Gnostic Gospels*) and Qumran (*Dead Sea Scrolls*) predate the texts (*Matthew, Mark, Luke,* and *John*) that were edited and synthesized (to form the core of what is known as the *New Testament*) by those seeking to separate Jesus and his teachings from Judaism— including the apostle Paul, Bishop Irenaeus of Lyon (3rd Century CE), and the Council of Nicaea (4th Century CE)—for the sake of Constantine's imperial exigencies (a means of controlling the masses).

[319] *Observations on: I. The Answer of M L'Abbé de Vertot to the late Earl Stanhope's Inquiry concerning the Senate of Ancient Rome, dated December 1719; II. A Dissertation upon the Constitution of the Roman Senate, by a Gentleman, published in 1743; III. A Treatise on the Roman Senate, by Dr. Conyers Middleton, published in 1747; IV. An Essay on the Roman Senate, by Dr. Thomas Chapman, published in 1750; by Mr. Hooke, published in 1758,* specifically "Observations of Dr. Middleton's Treatise and Dr. Chapman's Essay on the Roman Senate," p. 189.

Money, not capital, as currency: the prohibition of usury

Regarding interest, as we noted in *Step 1*, all three Abrahamic religions (Judaism, Christianity, and Islam) prohibit usury, and the reasons are obvious: interest is the antithesis of labor; it is fake value created without work; it turns money from a measure of the value created by labor into a commodity (capital) that is manipulated for its own sake, thereby tyrannizing labor, all of which necessarily results in the theft and devaluation of labor. So, in the images of the cleansing of the Temple, we see a spiritual figure in a religious setting taking direct action against economic behaviors that he considers to be both a crime against humanity (the devaluation of labor) and G-d (blasphemy).

If we are to transform the world from one that values capital (the golden calf, mammon, the almighty dollar, etc.) above all else into one that places people (labor) and all living things, as well as their support systems (the biosphere), at the center, then we must reformulate our economic and political dynamics so that money is a public utility; that is, money must be a tool to benefit the human race and its environment, rather than a commodity manipulated to enrich a few families and their minions.

Ending conflation of disparate forces and points-of-view

Prior to outlining the economic and political framework for such a society, in *Step 2* we dispelled a number of logical fallacies that impede clarity of thought and prevent us from conceiving a proper definition of terms, by noting that we must separate the objectives and behavior of the international banking cartel from any particular nation, religion, or ethnicity because, literally, many different groups have been coerced into contributing to the problem. "We have met the enemy and he is us," says Pogo, the swamp possum and title character in Walt Kelley's famous syndicated comic strip (1948-1975).

In the broadest spiritual and scientific sense, those committing the most heinous crimes on the planet are a reflection of our own shadows: our ego and our instincts untempered by the capacity which connects each of us to all other people and living things, and to the universe itself, via Singularity. As noted in *Step 2*, this selfish condition—the ascendancy of the shadow—holds true of all hostile parties in the Levant (the proxies for the cartel and the religious fundamentalists), as well as to those at the top of the power pyramid that we examined in *Step 3*.

Shining a light on the power elite

For most of us, *Step 3* may be the most challenging proposition, because it requires coming to grips with power beyond what we have imagined possible, all of which was enabled originally by private control over money creation. However, once past this hurdle, what we found intrinsic to the ruling elite is a set of beliefs that fall outside of the moral boundaries to which most of us subscribe. The cure for this amorality, we discovered, is the transfer of power over money creation, and sovereignty itself, back to the public sector, by reestablishing money as a public utility to be managed in the public interest.

In *Step 4*, we determined that the keys to accomplishing this monetary transformation is that we recognize: private banking is not a business, but a weapon of war and an instrument of theft; and, only a publicly owned banking network operating without usury can provide a stable currency and sustainable economy over the long term.

Further, as we discovered in *Step 5*, such a public banking network is not, in and of itself, sufficient to guarantee a sustainable progressive society, but must be accompanied, at a bare minimum, by verifiable voting and decentralized media.

A return to rationality

Finally, as we noted in *Step 6*, what the corporate-owned mass and social media, educational sectors (including scientific research), and the intelligence services hold up as rational and reasonable thought are—as are all such mainstream ideas and systems in a world commodified by capital—rife with logical fallacies that benefit private interests. Yet, despite the cartel's hubris in attempting to distort the framework and methodology of empirical reasoning, we know that models and hypotheses cannot "prove" anything, only venture to define processes supported by the given data, while additional data may invalidate any hypothesis or model.

The marriage of uncertainty and relativity

The achievement of employing empirical reasoning and producing scientific proof becomes even more difficult when Heisenberg's Uncertainty Principle is reconciled with Relativity; for example, take the quantum observation that the experimenter appears to affect the experiment (i.e., "When you look for the particle, you see the particle; when you look for the wave, you see the wave.") and, contra-positively, light is perceived as being a wave and a particle at the same time. How can light manifest two separate states of matter simultaneously?

This quandary led Heisenberg to go so far as to say:

> "Perhaps it is not too rash to hope that new spiritual forces will again bring us nearer to the unity of a scientific concept of the universe ..."[320]; and,

> "The advance from the parts already completed to those newly discovered, or to be newly erected, demands each time an

---

[320] Heisenberg, Werner, *Philosophic Problems of Nuclear Science*, Fawcett Premier Books, New York, 1952, p. 28.

intellectual jump, which cannot be achieved through the simple development of already existing knowledge."[321]

Pushing the envelope of logic

Einstein and Heisenberg were theoretical physicists whose realm is far beyond rocket science and brain surgery; their work pushes the envelope of logic as we know it—where Singularity, String Theory, Poincaire's Conjecture,[322] and so-called imaginary numbers[323] comprise the vocabulary for describing the universe.

As noted at the top of this chapter, in this realm, the scientific concept of Singularity—everything that ever was, is, or will be—appears identical to the generic concept of Deity—omniscience, omnipotence, and omnipresence. This is the convergence point for science and spirituality: they both point to a state or dimension of the universe in which total unity is the only property. The bottom line is this: whether we choose to frame our world in scientific or spiritual terminology, the result is the same: everything in the universe was once (and continues to be, via the 1st dimension) the very same thing, and that very same thing—Singularity or G-d whatever you choose to call it—is what engenders the infinite variations of the universe, including economics and spirituality. In other words, these two seemingly disparate fields

---

[321] *Ibid.*, p. 27.

[322] In lay terms, the conjecture proves that three-dimensional space is reducible to spheres and doughnuts, which makes it congruent to proving that all four-dimensional space is reducible to a torus (i.e., a four-dimensional sphere-doughnut).

[323] Previously, imaginary numbers were defined as a class of numbers or quantity expressed in terms of the square root of a negative number (usually the square root of -1); however, just as we have discovered, through Heisenberg's Uncertainty Principle, that light may be a particle and a wave at the same time, so then may the square root of -1 be both +1 and -1; i.e., not imaginary numbers, but positive and negative integers, or states, if you prefer. In this way are the logical propositions of mathematics brought into alignment with Relativity and Uncertainty.

188

are inextricably bound in the most fundamental of ways and, in particular, on the question of interest, as illustrated by the story of Jesus cleansing the temple of usurers ("Thieves!").

From Homo Economus to Homo Spiritus

So, retracing the logical progression of our argument, we now have advanced our analysis from the most materialistic realm, that of money and economics, to that of the most sublime—that which we hold in our hearts and minds. While we submit that there are infinite possibilities for proving our thesis, we find precedence for our argument from an approach to the history of political thought as taught by Charles A. Drekmeier,[324] Emeritus Professor of Political Science at Stanford University, whose introductory syllabus proceeded through the theoretical and practical history of this discipline in chronological order until it reached the 18th and 19th centuries, where he reversed the order of three key thinkers:

$$Marx \longrightarrow Hegel \longrightarrow Rousseau$$

Drekmeier's larger point is this: If we aim to make human evolution our objective, then we must understand our own hierarchy of needs (to borrow a phrase from Abraham Maslow) and the order in which to fulfill them.

The Hierarchy of Needs

Thus, after our step-by-step progression, advancing from Marx's social reality (Maslow's physiological and instinctive safety factors) to Hegel's psychological ideals (Maslow's love/belonging and esteem),

---

[324] The author's advisor in Political Science at Stanford University.

we have arrived at Rousseau's existential questions regarding what Maslow calls humankind's self-actualization.

Overcoming the tyranny of the instincts and ego

Stepping outside of western philosophy and psychology and looking at this from an eastern point-of-view, the challenges we face in fulfilling our hierarchy of needs and achieving self-actualization involve our ability, individually and collectively, to develop a conscious state free from the tyranny of the instincts and the ego.

Conscious spiritual evolution

In our first book, *Solomon's Proof—A Psycho-Spiritual Journey to World Consciousness*,[325] written under the pen name of Rashan Barcusé, we introduced our framework for the final theory, which defines the next step in human development as "conscious spiritual evolution,"[326] as well as devoted an entire chapter to a dialogue concerning selected eastern and western (Yoga and psychology) approaches to such self-actualization.

What is to be gained from the convergence of spiritual practice and psychology?

The idea of combining eastern and western approaches to the liberation of consciousness and the evolution of human behavior has been around since the Orient and the Occident first interacted, in much the same way as the two hemispheres of the brain interact to mix acausal[327] and causal

---

[325] http://www.amazon.com/Solomons-Proof-Rashan-Barcuse/dp/0615185371

[326] An updated version of this framework is available at
http://www.solomonsproof.com

[327] We use the term in the sense defined by Carl G. Jung's discussion in *Synchronicity: An Acausal Connecting Principle* (1952) and elsewhere.

reasoning; that is, combining space and time into one concept. Of course, such four-dimensional mental alchemy does not guarantee a useful synthesis of ideas that serve as a springboard for human evolution. For that, we must make a concerted effort to cull the intellectual and spiritual wheat from the chaff.

Where we stand

However, before we do that, let's revisit the present gap between our objectives (the ultimate measure our success) and our present state:

Step 1 — Exposing the story of money and usury: While there is a growing public banking movement, the public banks that do exist remain under attack worldwide by the private banking cartel. As noted in *Step 4*, the cartel is seeking to prohibit public banking through a variety of means, including treaties, such as TPP and TTIP and their reiterative progeny, which would also codify the private banks and their corporations as sovereign over nations and states. In addition, the corporate controlled media and educational system almost never discuss economics outside the box of a privately owned system of money creation. Thus, the corporate-controlled state reinforces the status quo, including an emphasis on ego, self-interest, and materialism, and impedes evolution in the process.

Step 2 — Rejecting the false divisions of ethnicities, religions, political parties, and nationalities: Creating and exacerbating divisions between different groups of human beings remains a key strategy for the cartel, because it fulfills many of their objectives at once, including war profiteering, population reduction, and struggle-for-survival as a distraction from the root cause of global dysfunction (private control over money creation). One of the standard tactics to create animosities is to use *agent provocateurs*, saboteurs, dupes, and "Manchurian Candidates" to perform violent acts for which one side or another is blamed. The cartel is also willing to spend a little money to create and maintain strong, misleading brand identities; for example, gay rights (an important issue) has been adopted by the blue party, whose constituents confuse equality with freedom, not seeing that equal slaves to the cartel is still inequality and certainly not freedom.

> "A society that puts equality before freedom will get neither. A society that puts freedom before equality will get a high degree of both."[328] —Milton Friedman

Step 3 — Transposing the money cartel's point-of-view: While one of the key *modi operandi* of the cartel is slaughter on a vast scale, it is important, in attempting to take the next evolutionary step, that we do not fall for the notion that revolutionary violence will get us there. As an alternative, we should look beyond the various political revolutions of the past to a revolution of human consciousness and behavior that manifests the change, through its continued focus on the root cause.

Consider the great novelist and social reformer Charles Dickens. Of all his great works, his personal favorite was *A Christmas Carol*. In this story, Dickens chose to frame his antagonist/protagonist, Ebenezer Scrooge, as a usurer from the City of London, the independent political body run by the world's largest banks in the heart of the British empire. While Scrooge is generally remembered for his scornful disposition— "Bah, humbug!" and "If they (the poor) would rather die, they had better do it, and decrease the surplus population."—in fact, it is his personal transformation (epiphany) that is the climax of Dickens' story.

And what was it that got Scrooge to evolve? Four ghosts, each of whom focused on specific events past, present, and future in Scrooge's life.

This is not to say, even if massive numbers of people stood in witness to the crimes of the banking cartel, that the individuals at the top of the

---

[328] From *Created Equal*, an episode of the PBS *Free to Choose* television series (1980, vol. 5 transcript).

power pyramid would suddenly gain insight into their own sociopathic and psychopathic behavior; nevertheless, such a strategy is an important part of a larger effort. It is we, the people, who play the role of the ghosts—our ancestors, as it were. This is why the powers-that-be violently shut down Native American ghost dances in the late 19th Century—out of fear of their own subconscious guilt, just as with Scrooge. It is these subconscious ghosts of human conscience that we must summon to the fore and with which we must come to terms, in order to evolve. Like Dickens, we are telling a ghost story, resurrecting ancient powers derived from light.

Step 4 — Making money a public utility through sustainable economics: As we show in this chapter, a progressive society and sustainable economy is only possible through local, regional, national (and, eventually, international) networks of public banks that create and regulate money based on the value created by labor and its adjuncts (machines, computers, robots, and artificial intelligence), and doing so without turning the accounting for labor (money) into a commodity (capital); that is, by enforcing the prohibition of usury. As it stands today, despite the success of public banks—particularly in Switzerland and Germany—the cartel continues to make inroads (via war and subterfuge) in privatizing public banks, in Japan, New Zealand, and BRICS,[329] as well as suppressing any nascent activity in the U.S., Canada, and elsewhere.

Step 5 — Restoring democracy: WWIII is taking place right now. It is "the endless war on terror," which is more accurately described as the endless war of corporate-state sponsored terrorism, as well as an

---

[329] Brazil, Russia, India, China, and South Africa.

information war, against the people.[330] No more than a half-dozen companies continue to control the mass media in the U.S.[331]

Step 6 — Restoring law, science, and logic: The cartel also uses its control over the corporate and governmental sectors, including intelligence and military services, to extend its reach over thought—including law, science, and logic—by dictating the limits of public discourse and education. For example: laws that violate the Constitution and the Bill of Rights are enforceable only because the judiciary is owned and operated by the cartel; so-called climate scientists (subsidized by government and corporate grants that are disbursed with the *quid pro quo* that the results adhere to the Party line) draw a direct cause and effect relationship between the use of fossil fuels and the database of global warming statistics without ever considering the complicity of intelligence and military services via manipulation of the database, as well as through the big white elephant in the room—the use of weather-as-a-weapon to create drought, floods, and catastrophic events (as we documented in *Step 3*).[332]

Integrating meditation and psychology to strengthen our resolve

So, in the face of a seemingly monolithic force that uses its considerable resources to block every substantive initiative that

---

[330] For example, when the cartel uses its hegemony over mass media, polling organizations, state legislatures (to promulgate gerrymandering and voter suppression), and the Congress (to promulgate limitless campaign financing) to create the plausible illusion of neck-and-neck elections, which are then stolen via electronic voting machines. The 2016 primary and general elections are transparent expression of this criminal activity. See our analysis at: http://coloradopublicbanking.blogspot.com/2016/11/the-2016-selection.html

[331] https://www.rt.com/op-edge/158920-us-ukraine-media-control/

[332] http://www.geoengineeringwatch.org/massive-us-senate-document-on-national-and-global-weather-modification/

threatens its power, we find that we must integrate spiritual practice and psychology to strengthen our resolve to continue to educate and initiate actions that challenge the cartel's affront to human potentiality and to the evolutionary forces intrinsic in light itself, of which the universe is wholly comprised.

Beyond dogma and logical fallacies

There are those who deny such a through line to the universe, either out of servitude to the cartel, or out of ignorance, or from a lack of comprehension of the data before us, including adherence to various systems of dogma and logical fallacies,[333] as we have evidenced in the first six steps.

Leaving these obsolete thought patterns behind us clears the way for many models, past and present, particularly those of indigenous tribes, that exemplify sharing and other conscious evolutionary behaviors; for example, the African philosophy of Ubuntu,[334] which declines to exclude any member of the group from the success of the whole. Perhaps this is why the sociopaths and psychopaths who control the majority of the world's resources have made such a concerted effort to wipe out native and aboriginal societies—because, without enforced scarcity and consumer addictions based on the tyranny of the ego and instincts, their control over the planet would dissolve.

So, given the contextual status of our first six steps, what is the next step in human evolution?

While a number of actions are needed by large numbers of people (whatever the tipping point may be), our next step begins with each of

---

[333] https://yourlogicalfallacyis.com/

[334] http://www.trueactivist.com/gab_gallery/an-anthropologist-proposed-a-game-to-children-in-an-african-tribe/

us having some form of spiritual practice. We call it spiritual because it involves activating our higher selves; that is, self-actualization: a qualitatively different state of being when compared to where most of us find ourselves today.

What is spiritual practice and what are its parameters?

A spiritual practice can be as simple as taking a deep breath and counting to ten before speaking or acting on instinctive or egoistic impulses, or it can be as involved and multi-layered as the eight limbs of Yoga, but the objective of any bona fide spiritual practice is overcoming the tyranny of the instincts and the ego and learning to share; that is, creating a center of consciousness that is unencumbered by hormonal urges and "the small self" of the frontal lobes. Any practice which fails to accomplish these basic transformational experiences for its practitioners condemns them to the state we find our rulers trying to instill and justify today, in order to maintain the status quo—that of greed, self-interest, and profiting at the expense of our neighbors. As the quote from W.H. Auden, at the beginning of this chapter declares, "We must love one another or die." Sharing is fundamental to this evolutionary step.

Be the change

As all the spiritual masters through the ages have taught, we must be the change that we envision. Non-violent protest[335] is, of course, encouraged, as we have iterated in *Step 5* and *Step 6*, but the foundation for the new world that we seek is an evolutionary as well as revolutionary upgrade of present institutions. It is in these

---

[335] Non-violence to persons is a must; but actions against property are a different matter because, in a capitalist/fascist system, most of what is owned by the .000001% is acquired via criminal activity.

196

transformational solutions that we are creating this foundation, first inside of ourselves, by pulling ourselves up by our own spiritual bootstraps (*Step 7*), and second, by extending this consciousness into the world, via our intentions, our envisioning of their manifestation (*Steps 1-6*), and our actions. These are the bridges to that new world, which is alive and growing as we speak. After all, as light conscious of itself, we possess the greatest power of all: all beings, regardless of the technology and power that they possess, have equal access to omnipresent source energy.

Discover your gift, develop it, and share it

All that is required to bring about this manifestation is for each of us to discover his and/or her unique gifts, develop those gifts, and share them with the world. This is what aligns us with the universe. Whether we represent this connectedness by words such as G-d or Singularity, or by some other symbolic form, it is now a tenet of the current cosmological model that everything in the universe comes from the very same thing. Sharing is the manifestation of this unity in humankind; that is, light is perfectly reflected via the heart.[336]

Peace be with you.

---

[336] www.solomonsproof.com

.

www.ingramcontent.com/pod-product-compliance
Lightning Source LLC
Chambersburg PA
CBHW030008290326
41934CB00005B/258